Misery Guts

MORRIS GLEITZMAN

Misery Guts

**Harcourt**

Orlando   Boston   Dallas   Chicago   San Diego

Visit *The Learning Site!*

www.harcourtschool.com

For my parents

Printed in the United States of America

ISBN   0-15-314409-2

2 3 4 5 6 7 8 9 10   060   03 02 01

Chapter One

Keith's heart was pounding.

Calm down, he thought. You're not robbing a bank. You're not kidnapping anybody. You're just painting a fish-and-chip shop orange.

He looked up and down his street, peering into the early-morning fog.

Everything was gray. Gray houses. Gray shops. Gray cars. Gray blocks of flats looming up into a gray sky.

The cold air was making his ears hurt.

This is why, he thought. This is why Mum and Dad are such misery guts. The weather.

He pulled his collar up around his ears. Thirty-five years of it was enough to give anyone a long

1

face. He'd only had twelve and a quarter years of it and even he got the willies sometimes.

Oh well, he thought, they'll be feeling better soon. When they see what I've done.

He looked at his watch. Seven-fifteen. Mum'll be awake soon. Dad'll be back from the market at eight.

And neither of them's got a clue they're about to be cheered up.

Keith grinned at the thought.

Then he turned back to the shop front, dipped his brush into the tin, and carried on painting.

The Tropical Mango Hi-Gloss spread over the dull brown of the window frame like liquid sunshine.

Keith's heart pounded even faster. It looked even better than he'd thought it would.

While he painted, he imagined Mum and Dad's faces when they saw it. The big grins spreading over both their faces. Those big droopy creases at the corners of Dad's mouth, gone. Those frown lines on Mum's forehead, vanished.

He stood on a soft-drink crate to reach the top bit of the window frame, brushing the Tropical Mango on as thickly as he could so not much of the brown showed through. When they see this, thought Keith, they'll think the sun's come out.

Then he heard the sound of a door slamming. He looked around. It wasn't the sun coming out, it was Mr. Naylor from next door.

Keith sighed. Here we go.

Mr. Naylor looked at the paint, at the brush, and at the Tropical Mango window frame.

"What are you doing?" he asked suspiciously.

Teaching sheep to juggle toasters, thought Keith, then remembered he'd promised Mum he wouldn't be cheeky to Mr. Naylor now he was twelve.

"Painting our shop. For Dad's birthday. It's a surprise."

Mr. Naylor gave the window frame a long stare.

"Won't dry in this weather," he said.

"It's quick-drying," said Keith. "You get a brilliant long-lasting finish in only hours. Says so on the tin."

"Horrible color," said Mr. Naylor.

"The man in the shop said orange reminds people of their summer holidays," said Keith.

"It's dripping on the pavement," said Mr. Naylor and shuffled away toward the bus stop.

Keith wondered when Mr. Naylor had last smiled. Eighteen forty-seven, probably.

He looked at the pavement. There were a few orange spots. He rubbed them with his foot, but they were already starting to go like old custard skin. Oh well, he thought, what's a bit of spotty pavement when you're bringing happiness to two people?

He moved on to the door. It was good to have a decent-sized flat bit to work on. He'd gone a bit wonky on the window frame in places.

He smoothed big brushfuls of paint on and had

3

a vision of Mum and Dad, big grins still on their faces, going over to Lewisham and buying themselves some colorful clothes and coming back and having a party for Dad's birthday. Just the three of them. Getting out all their old records, the Rolling Stones and stuff. Mum and Dad dancing. He'd never seen them dance.

The shop door glowed and so did Keith.

A hand reached past him and stuck a rolled-up newspaper in the letter box.

"Waste of time, that."

Keith sighed.

Mitch Wilson stepped around him and stuffed a paper into Mr. Naylor's letter box.

"Be filthy dirty in a week."

"Comes up like new with a simple wipe," said Keith. "Says so on telly."

Tragic, he thought, watching Mitch trying to stuff a wad of magazines through the door of the hairdresser two doors down. Only ten and he was as big a moaner as Mrs. Wall in the laundrette. She didn't even like people getting married in case the tablecloths from the reception put a strain on her driers.

"Be filthy dirty again in another week."

Keith didn't bother answering. No point with a moaner. And only two years ago Mitch Wilson had been an eager little kid who'd wanted to be a Mars Bar salesman.

Keith put the soft-drink crate on top of the dustbin and climbed up to do the sign over the window. Vin's Fish Supplies. He decided to do the background rather than the lettering. Do the lettering in Rainforest Green later.

As he slapped the paint on he wondered if there was an award for the Brightest Fish-and-Chip Shop in Britain. That'd really get Dad's eyes sparkling again. Princess Di dropping in to shake his hand and give him a solid silver cod fillet.

This thought was shattered by a whine.

Keith sighed.

Owen the milkman.

The whine was coming from the milk truck, but Owen soon started one of his own.

"That's not a color I'd have chosen, Keith. Show the dirt something awful, bright colors. Won't dry this time of year neither, gloss paint. Wife's cousin did their garage in November, still tacky in March. Tell your mum no yogurt till Thursday."

Owen's whine stopped, the truck's started, and he was gone.

No wonder Mum and Dad are depressed, thought Keith, with a milkman like that.

He finished off the sign and climbed down to get the full effect.

On the pavement he tried to imagine he was a depressed parent. He looked up at the glowing Tropical Mango and felt cheered up immediately. Then he half closed his eyes and banged himself on the head with his knuckles to see what it would look like with temporary bad eyesight due to a tension headache.

Not bad.

"Keith, what are you doing out here?"

Keith opened his eyes. Mum was standing next to him in her dressing gown, staring at the Tropical Mango. She stared at it for quite a long time. The frown lines on her forehead looked deeper than ever.

Keith, heart pounding, waited for her to be cheered up.

Instead she stared at him.

"It's a birthday surprise for Dad," he explained. "And you."

He wished she'd stop staring at him.

"Even though it's not your birthday," he added.

Please smile, Mum, he thought. Please don't turn into Mr. Naylor.

"It's to cheer you both up."

She didn't smile.

She stared back at the paint.

She closed her eyes and held them closed for ages.

Must be the paint fumes, he thought. Funny though, they didn't sting my eyes.

She looked at him again.

"Keith."

Her voice sounded funny. Could paint fumes affect the vocal cords?

"Where did you get the paint?"

"Sally Prescott gave me eleven quid for my stamp collection."

She breathed out slowly and her face softened a bit.

At last.

But she still didn't smile.

"Keith," she said, "I don't think you should be around when Dad gets back."

Keith was confused. Surely she wasn't planning to pinch the birthday surprise? Pretend it was from her? Not Mum. Not the woman who'd sat up with him all night after he'd seen *Nightmare on Elm Street*.

Before he could tell her he'd go fifty-fifty and that was his final offer, Dad came around the corner in the van and pulled up in front of the shop.

Keith stepped forward.

"Happy birthday, Dad. From me and Mum."

Dad sat behind the wheel, motionless, staring up at the shop, mouth open.

Keith opened the van door in case the surprise had sapped Dad's strength.

"Vin," said Mum, "before you say anything, Keith's done this as a birthday present. Just try and remember that, love, he did it as a birthday present."

All right, Mum, thought Keith, don't overdo it, I think he's got the message.

He waited for Dad to take it all in. For Dad's face to light up with the sheer joy of the Tropical Mango

7

Hi-Gloss. And then for him to throw back his head and roar with delighted laughter.

Or even just give a big grin, like he did in that photo when he won Best Fish-and-Chips at the Woolwich Show before Keith was born.

Or a smile.

Half a smile.

Keith realized Dad was staring down at the pavement.

Then he looked at Keith with an expression that made Mr. Naylor, Mitch Wilson, and Owen the milkman look like the happiest people on earth.

"Inside," he said.

Chapter Two

It's got to stop, Keith."

Keith stared at the back of the cornflakes box on the kitchen table. A happy mum, a happy dad, and a happy kid were all playing happily with an inflatable beach ball they'd got by sending in two box tops and four pounds ninety-nine.

"Did you hear what I said?" demanded Dad. "It's got to stop."

Keith looked up at Dad's face. Dad's mouth was droopier than ever.

He looked up at Mum's face. Her forehead looked like she'd put some tucks in it with the sewing machine.

Keith sighed. They looked like they'd sent in two

box tops and four pounds ninety-nine and got back an inflatable dog poo.

"I'm just trying to cheer you both up," he said.

"Well, it's not working," said Dad.

Keith wondered if the *Guinness Book of Records* had a category for The Most Incredibly Obvious Statement Ever Made.

"That business a few weeks ago," continued Dad. "Did you honestly think drawing funny faces on the cod fillets with tomato sauce was going to make us dance with joy?"

Not dance with joy, thought Keith. Have a bit of a giggle perhaps.

"Mrs. Wall nearly had a heart attack," said Mum. "She thought we'd left the heads on them."

"And rigging up the record player under our bed," said Dad. "Me and Mum might be strange, but having the living daylights scared out of us doesn't leave us feeling very cheerful."

"I thought you liked the Rolling Stones," said Keith.

"Not at six o'clock in the morning," said Mum, "and not that loud. Mr. Naylor thought the fryer in the shop had exploded."

"And now this," said Dad. "It's . . . it's . . ."

Keith watched him trying to find the words, pacing around the kitchen.

All right, thought Keith, it's not the best paint job

in the world, but it's not bad considering. If Picasso had done his painting in the freezing cold without gloves he'd have dripped a bit and gone over the edges too.

Dad turned to face him.

"Why?" he said. "That's what I don't understand. Why this obsession with cheering us up?"

"It's not as if we're in mourning or anything," said Mum. "Nobody's died. We haven't been robbed. The shop hasn't burned down."

"So why all this nonsense about cheering us up?" said Dad. "Just answer me that. Why?"

• • •

First period at school was science and Keith managed to have a quiet word with Mr. Crouch, the science teacher.

"Sir," said Keith, "you know all those science magazines you read, what's the latest research data on cheerful people who have to live with misery guts?"

Mr. Crouch, who was reading a gardening magazine, looked at him suspiciously.

"How do you mean?"

"Well," said Keith, "if a person who's still pretty cheerful has to live with people who aren't cheerful anymore, what's the average amount of time it takes for the cheerful person to end up a misery guts too?"

Mr. Crouch told him to go back to his seat and finish boiling his tap water.

• • •

At lunchtime Keith managed to have another quiet word with Mr. Crouch.

"Sir, you know how we've just been boiling up tap water to find the impurities and stuff?"

"Distillation," said Mr. Crouch through a mouthful of peanut butter sandwich. "It's in your textbook."

"I was just wondering, sir," said Keith, "if there's any research been done on whether impurities in tap water can turn people into misery guts."

"Go away," said Mr. Crouch, turning the page of his rose catalog, "I'm busy."

"How about rays from the TV?" said Keith. "I read somewhere once that TVs give out rays that can make people depressed if they're not getting enough sleep. Either that or microwave ovens."

Mr. Crouch put down his catalog and his sandwich, stood up, gripped Keith by the shoulder, and steered him across the staff room and out into the corridor. Then he went back into the staff room and closed the door.

Keith put his mouth to the keyhole.

"How about the greenhouse effect?"

• • •

It was still foggy when Keith walked home from school, but as he turned the corner into his street he could see the Tropical Mango glowing through the fog even at that distance.

He felt a tingle of pleasure.

If it can make me feel good at fifty yards, he thought, it's got to work on them at less than ten feet.

He hurried home to see if Mum and Dad were smiling yet.

They were waiting for him in the shop.

They weren't smiling.

"Son," said Dad, "we've decided the time's come to tell you what's what."

Eh? thought Keith. What does he mean?

It couldn't be where baby cod come from, they'd done that ages ago.

"You're right, Keith," said Mum, "me and Dad aren't the happy-go-lucky people we used to be."

"And there are reasons for that," said Dad, "and we want you to know what they are. So you'll stop all this nonsense."

Keith's insides felt as though they'd just dropped several hundred feet into a bowl of cold batter.

What were they going to tell him? What awful things didn't he know about?

He stared at Mum and Dad, hardly daring to look for the telltale signs of brain tumors or fatal diseases you could get from handling too much raw fish.

13

Dad lifted a big sack of flour onto the counter. And a big drum of fat. He didn't look as if he was suffering from anything too bad.

"Do you know what this is?" he asked.

Keith nodded. "Fat and flour."

Dad lifted a sack of potatoes onto the counter and took a block of fish from the freezer.

"And this?"

Oh no, thought Keith, don't tell me Dad's banged his head on the fryer hood and forgotten the basic ingredients of fish-and-chips.

"Fish and potatoes," he said. "The potatoes are the round ones."

"Not just any fat and flour and fish and potatoes," said Dad. "Cheap fat and cheap flour and cheap fish and cheap potatoes."

Keith realized with a shock there was a wobble in Dad's voice.

"The sort of fat and flour and fish and potatoes I said I'd never use. When I started this shop before you were born I only used the best vegetable oil and the best matzo flour and the freshest fish and the best potatoes. I used to turn out the best fish-and-chips in South London. I don't anymore and that's why I don't spend much time cracking jokes and kicking up my heels."

Before Keith could ask Dad why he didn't cheer himself up by going back to turning out the best fish-

and-chips in South London, Mum and Dad were steering him up the stairs and into the flat.

They stopped in the little hallway that ran between his bedroom and Mum and Dad's bedroom.

"When we got married," said Mum, "me and Dad had wonderful plans. We were going to live here for a few years, and have you, which we did, and then buy a house, and then have a little brother or sister for you."

Keith stared at her. How many times when he was a kid, when he still said his prayers, had he asked God for a brother or sister? Fifty at least. Almost as many times as he'd asked for a helicopter.

"Why didn't you?" he asked. Now the wobble was in his voice.

Mum took a deep breath. Keith noticed she was squeezing Dad's hand very hard.

"Because we couldn't afford to, love. The shop wasn't earning us enough money."

"It would have done if Dad had kept on turning out the best fish-and-chips in South London," said Keith, turning to Dad. "Wouldn't it?"

"When we started the shop," said Dad, "there was us and one curry place down the street. Now there's us and three curry places and McDonald's and Kentucky Fried and Spud-U-Like and the pub bistro and two other fish-and-chip shops."

"The only way we can make a living is to keep

our prices down," said Mum. "And cheap prices mean cheap ingredients. And no money left over for houses." She bit her lip.

Keith frowned.

"But we sell loads of fish-and-chips, mountains of them. There must be enough money to rent a house at least."

Dad looked at him grimly.

"Life's not that simple, son. There's tax and electricity bills and repairs to the shop and repairs to the fryers and repayments on the new fridge and insurance in case Mrs. Wall slips in a puddle of vinegar and council fees and government fees and every time there's a flood anywhere the price of potatoes goes through the roof."

Keith looked at Dad. No wonder his mouth was droopy.

He looked at Mum. No wonder her forehead looked like Auntie Joyce's peasant-smock party dress.

Then Dad gripped him by both shoulders.

"I'm afraid that life," said Dad, "is not a lot of fun."

"So, love," said Mum, "do you understand now?"

"Yes," said Keith.

Chapter Three

Keith lay in bed planning his next move.

He thought about digging up the pavement outside the shop and planting daffodils. Everyone liked daffs. Even people who didn't like Tropical Mango Hi-Gloss. Even Mum and Dad.

The council wouldn't though.

He had a vision of a council bulldozer arriving and bulldozing all the daffs and him having to jump onto the bulldozer driver from the kitchen window and wrestle him to the ground and . . .

Scrap that idea.

Okay, what about a holiday? A camping trip. Borrow Uncle Derek's tent. Go somewhere exotic. Dennis Baldwin and his parents went to Dorset last year.

Dad could visit all the Dorset fish-and-chip shops and make some pen pals.

Keith started working out how long it would take him to earn enough for a camping holiday in Dorset.

He'd just calculated that the two pence a potato Mum and Dad paid him meant he'd have to peel at least ten thousand potatoes when he remembered that Dennis Baldwin had come home from Dorset six days early last year because his mum had hit his dad over the head with a deck chair.

Scrap that idea.

I know, he thought, I'll ring up a circus and invite them to tea on Sunday. Not a whole circus, just some jugglers and clowns and a baby elephant . . .

He remembered Mum was allergic to straw.

Then Keith's bedroom door creaked open and someone came into the room.

It was Dad.

Great, thought Keith, here am I trying to come up with ways to cheer them up, and Dad remembers another thing to be miserable about. What will it be this time? The pipe in the kitchen that bangs when you turn the hot tap off too quickly? His team's run of fourteen games away without a win? The government?

Dad sat down on the edge of the bed. In the darkness Keith could just make out his mouth.

Funny, thought Keith, it's not drooping.

"Son," said Dad, and cleared his throat. "Thanks for the birthday present. I've got to be honest and say I'd rather have had a pair of socks, but it's the thought that counts."

Keith couldn't believe it.

Right up to bedtime Dad had been sighing and shaking his head and muttering how it should be illegal to sell Tropical Mango Hi-Gloss to kids under eighteen.

What had happened?

Keith was still wondering when Dad leaned forward and did something even more surprising.

He gave Keith a hug.

Keith hugged him back, heart thumping, trying to remember the last time they'd done this.

What had happened?

Then he remembered.

The cake.

• • •

When he'd given Dad his birthday cake earlier, Dad had just stared at it.

At first Keith had thought Dad didn't want it. Perhaps he didn't want to be reminded he was thirty-five. Perhaps he knew Keith had forgotten to wash his hands before making it. Perhaps he was allergic to iced chocolate sponge cake in the shape of a haddock.

Then Dad had given Keith a big slap on the back and said all sorts of stuff about what a great cake it was and how clever Keith was.

But he hadn't actually smiled.

Now Keith looked at Dad through the darkness.

"Did you really like the cake?" he asked.

He strained to see Dad's expression in the gloom.

Dad's lips moved.

Keith's heart leapt.

Was that a . . . ?

It was.

Dad was smiling.

"That," said Dad, "was a great cake."

The smile slowly faded.

"Hope you didn't put too much sugar in. I'll be up all night burping if you did."

Before Keith could say he'd only put six cups in, Dad squeezed his arm and was gone.

Keith lay there, heart thumping.

It was a start.

• • •

Keith had the idea later that night.

He slipped out of bed, crept into the hall, and peeped into Mum and Dad's room.

All the lights were out.

He crept into the living room, fumbled around in the sideboard drawer till he found the flashlight, then shone it into the bottom of the cupboard behind the TV.

There it was.

The slide projector.

He dragged it out, blew the dust off it, and plugged it in. Then he piled the phone books onto the table, stood the projector on them, and fiddled with the focus.

A big square of white light appeared on the wall.

Now, he thought, the slides.

He went back to the cupboard with the flashlight and rummaged around. An old brown vase toppled and fell. Keith caught it inches from the floor.

That's all I need, he thought, Dad storming out here with a rolled-up umbrella thinking we're being burgled.

He found the plastic boxes of slides and hunted through them for a box taken in the days when Mum and Dad still laughed.

An old one.

He found one marked Holidays.

He knew that must be old, they hadn't had a holiday since he was about five.

Keith loaded the slides into the projector.

Click.

Him, huge on the wall, about three and a half, falling off a merry-go-round. That blur in the corner must be Dad, thought Keith.

21

Click.

Him, on a beach with a plastic bucket on his head.

Click.

Him, sitting on a donkey, dripping ice cream onto its neck.

Click. Click. Click.

Slides, swings, merry-go-round.

All him.

The only sign of Mum or Dad was an occasional arm or a couple of legs.

Keith switched the flashlight back on and found an even older-looking slide box. He loaded the slides.

Click.

Mum and Dad, incredibly young, with longer hair and really bright jumpers, posing in front of a castle with serious expressions on their faces.

Serious expressions, Keith noticed, but no frown lines or droop lines.

Click.

Dad, the same age, posing with a platter of fish-and-chips. A red sash across his chest. Smiling.

Click.

Mum and Dad, sitting at a table in an outdoor restaurant on some sort of seaside pier. Arms around each other. Heads thrown back. Eyes sparkling.

Laughing.

Keith stared.

Then he noticed something else in the slide. The

big flat fish on Mum and Dad's plates. And he remembered seeing the slide before, ages ago, when he was little. He'd asked Dad what the funny fish were called.

Dad had told him.

Dover sole.

"Dover sole," said Keith now, out loud, as he looked at Mum and Dad's laughing faces.

They must really have liked Dover sole.

He looked at the slide for a few minutes more, then leaned over to switch the projector off. He'd seen what he needed to see.

He bumped the slide box and it fell to the floor with a crash.

Keith looked anxiously toward Mum and Dad's room.

But it wasn't in Mum and Dad's room that the eruption of blankets took place.

It was on the settee.

Out of the darkness rose a crumpled figure, eyes screwed up, hair spiky, face twisted into a grimace.

Keith gasped. The blood pounded in his ears.

The figure's head was in the bright square of light on the wall.

Keith couldn't see who the head belonged to at first because Dad's laughing face was projected on top of it.

Then he saw who it was.

Dad.

He wasn't laughing.

• • •

Keith lay in bed and stared into the darkness.

He tried to think of pleasant things like how Dad, when he'd calmed down, had been quite reasonable about Keith looking at slides at one in the morning.

"Next time you can't sleep," Dad had said, "make do with a cup of hot milk, okay?"

Firm but fair, Keith had thought at the time. In between heart palpitations from the shock of Dad's appearance.

Now Keith's heart was beating fast for another reason.

Things were worse than he'd thought.

Mum and Dad didn't want to sleep together anymore.

He had to move fast.

Chapter Four

Keith stood in a puddle of fishy water, waiting.

Come on, Mr. Gossage, he thought. Shake a leg. Some of us have got to be at school in thirty-eight minutes.

All around him the fish market was a confusion of activity. Lorries and vans and piles of crates and people shouting and blowing their horns. Everyone in a hurry. Except Mr. Gossage, who stood behind the rippled glass of his office door like a frozen cod with a phone to its ear.

Keith's hands were numb with the cold. He blew on them and stuck them into his pockets and jingled his life savings. Four pounds eighty-three. Two hundred and forty-one and a half potatoes.

Wonder why Dover sole are so expensive, he

thought. Must be 'cause they're so flat. Good for sandwiches.

He hoped two hundred and forty-one and a half potatoes would be enough.

The office door opened and Mr. Gossage came out.

"Okay, sunshine," he boomed, "what can I do for you?"

"Two Dover sole, please," said Keith. "Freshest you've got."

"Two boxes of sole coming up," said Mr. Gossage. "Bit posh for your dad, isn't it?"

"Not two boxes," said Keith, "two fish."

Mr. Gossage looked at him.

"Sorry, my old son, I'm a wholesaler. Can't split a box. Wholesalers don't split boxes or they wouldn't be wholesalers, would they? Try a fishmonger."

He went back into the office.

"Our fishmonger doesn't have Dover sole," shouted Keith.

"Try Selfridges," shouted Mr. Gossage, picking up the phone, "or Dover."

Keith walked gloomily away. Selfridges was halfway across London and mega-posh with it. Two hundred and forty-one and a half potatoes didn't get you a bag of chips up there. They wore diamond rings on their fish fingers up there.

Oops, he thought, that's me nearly being a moaner. Think positive.

He thought positive. Perhaps he could get away

with flattening a couple of mackerel between bricks.

Then he saw it.

It was propped up on top of a box of whitebait. At first Keith thought it was plastic, but as he got closer he saw it was real.

It was the color of sunsets and tropical reefs and all of Auntie Joyce's lipsticks shimmering together. Each scale was a different color and when Keith moved his head a fraction, each scale was a different color again.

It was the most beautiful fish he'd ever seen.

He imagined Mum and Dad seeing it. Their jaws dropping and their eyes widening as they opened the fridge and found themselves staring at a thousand shimmering pastel colors.

Forget Dover sole.

Forget mackerel with stretch marks.

If this fish didn't cheer Mum and Dad up, nothing would.

Gripping his two hundred and forty-one and a half potatoes, Keith pushed through the circle of onlookers to ask how much.

· · ·

"Twenty-five quid? For a fish?"

Dennis Baldwin looked at Keith as though he was a lunatic or a West Ham supporter or something. Then he went back to what he was doing.

CRASH.

Keith sighed.

It wasn't easy, trying to have a sensible conversation with someone who was more interested in smashing a supermarket trolley into a phone box.

"Five quid each," said Keith. "Take it in turns. You'll all get your money's worth."

"Waste of time trying to cheer my mum and dad up," said Eric Cox, as he started his run-up with the trolley. "I've tried."

CRASH.

Sally Prescott gripped the trolley. "All mums and dads are depressed," she said.

"No, they're not," said Keith.

" 'Course they are," she said, taking aim. "When was the last time you saw a mum or a dad having a really good time? Like they used to when they were kids."

CRASH.

"Get your head examined," said Rami Smith.

"Save your money," said Mitch Wilson.

"I've got it," said Dennis Baldwin. "Buy your dad a fish finger and paint it orange."

CRASH.

Keith sighed.

•　•　•

Uncle Derek sighed.

"Look at that," he said, handing Keith a small

brown plastic box. "Supposed to be British work-manship."

Keith looked at the box.

"Hundreds of quid for a remote-control garage door," said Uncle Derek, "and the remote-control unit doesn't work."

"I bet if you give it a prod with a screwdriver it'll work," said Auntie Joyce.

"The screwdriver's in the garage," said Uncle Derek through gritted teeth, "and I can't get the garage door open."

Keith wondered if Uncle Derek had forgotten what they were meant to be talking about.

"Bradley. Diana. Get your feet off the furniture," snapped Uncle Derek.

Keith watched as his cousins took about half an hour to get their feet off the leather settee. He gave them a sympathetic shrug. They stuck their tongues out at him.

Tragic, thought Keith, only seven and nine, a bed-room each with fitted carpet, and they're like Uncle Derek already.

"So," said Uncle Derek, "what do you want to spend twenty-five quid on your dad for?"

"His birthday," said Keith.

Uncle Derek stared at him.

"His birthday?"

Uncle Derek pulled a small black plastic box from

his pocket, punched a few buttons, and glared at the screen.

"Eighty-nine quid for a computerized pocket organizer and it can't even remember a birthday. This country's going down the toilet."

"It's Japanese," said Auntie Joyce.

"They're just as bad," said Uncle Derek.

Auntie Joyce picked up Uncle Derek's wallet.

"Don't worry about paying us back," she said to Keith, "just put our names on the card."

• • •

Keith stood in the deserted market, shivering.

He wasn't sure if it was the cold or the excitement.

He watched the man wrap the fish in newspaper. The man handed him the bundle and he handed the man twenty-five pounds.

"By the way," said the man, "don't eat it, it's a bit old."

Eat it, thought Keith as he hurried to the bus stop. Eat a fish that cost one thousand two hundred and fifty potatoes? Fat chance.

It was going in the freezer. Then, in the years to come, whenever Mum and Dad were down in the dumps, he could get it out, give it a wipe, and watch the smiles spread across their faces.

• • •

He didn't put it in the freezer straight away.

He put it in the fridge because he wanted to surprise them. Sometimes they didn't open the freezer for days, but they opened the shop fridge about once every five minutes.

Five minutes passed.

They didn't open the fridge.

Keith hovered around the back of the shop watching Dad fillet some plaice and Mum mix up some batter.

He stared at the back of Dad's head and tried sending him an urgent telepathic message.

Open the fridge.

Dad scratched his bottom.

Keith decided he'd better try something else.

He closed his eyes and made a wish.

I wish, he thought, that someone would walk into the shop now and ask Dad for something in the fridge.

It was worth a try. Even though none of the other forty-six thousand nine hundred and ninety-nine wishes he'd made in his life had come true.

The shop door opened and a man in a suit came in carrying a clipboard.

"Afternoon, sir, afternoon, madam," said the man. "Health inspection. Shall we start with the fridge?"

Keith grinned. Forty-seven thousandth time lucky.

Dad and Mum exchanged weary looks and Dad came over and opened the fridge.

Keith watched as Dad stopped and stared. The fish sat on the middle shelf, shimmering. Mum came over and she and Dad stood side by side, mouths slowly opening.

Keith didn't say anything. He waited for the amazed delight to creep over their faces.

The health inspector joined them. He bent down, head close to the fish.

Keith grinned. What did he think it was, plastic?

"How old's this fish?" asked the health inspector.

Keith stopped grinning. Everyone was looking at him. No one was looking amazed or delighted.

"Um, four or five days, I think," he said. "It was flown in from abroad for a big hotel and they sent it back to the market 'cause it was the wrong sort. Perhaps a week."

The health inspector sniffed the fish again.

Why's he doing that, wondered Keith. Does he think we're going to eat it?

Keith turned to Mum and Dad. "Aren't the colors great?" he said. He had the awful thought that perhaps Mum and Dad were color blind and had forgotten to tell him.

The health inspector straightened up.

"If the next time I look that fish isn't there," he said slowly, "I won't have to issue a summons for having stale fish on the premises, will I?"

No, thought Keith, you won't. 'Cause in a month's time when you're back it won't be there. It'll be in the freezer.

Then suddenly Keith had the fish in his hands. Dad had snatched it out of the fridge and thrust it at him.

Not now, thought Keith, wait till he's gone.

Dad put his face close to Keith's. It wasn't a happy face.

"Get it out of here," he said, in a voice that was so quiet it sent a shiver down Keith's spine. "Now."

Keith opened his mouth to explain to the health inspector that it was all a misunderstanding and that the fish wasn't stale stock, it was more of a dead pet.

But Dad spoke again, and his voice was much louder.

"Take it outside and get rid of it. NOW."

• • •

Keith stood in the drizzle, boiling.

Okay, he thought, that's it. Enough. Finish.

If Mum and Dad want to be misery guts, they can be misery guts. But they aren't turning me into one.

He stared at the gray houses and the gray shops and gray flats.

There must be somewhere in the world, he thought, where people are happy. Where mums and dads laugh, and sleep in the same bed, and paint

33

their fish-and-chip shops orange without worrying about a few splashes on the pavement.

He looked down at the fish. The thousand pastel colors twinkled through the raindrops that covered it.

Bet you come from a place like that, he thought.

Then he heard a voice.

"Told you it wouldn't dry in this weather."

Keith looked up.

Mr. Naylor was standing in the doorway, prodding the paint on the front of the shop with his finger. He showed Keith his orange fingertip.

"You'll have to scrape it all off and start again."

"Not me," said Keith. "I'm going abroad."

Chapter Five

Mrs. Lambert wasn't much help.

"Dunno," she said, peering at the fish.

Come on, thought Keith, you're a geography teacher, you must have some idea where it comes from.

"Looks tropical," said Mrs. Lambert, struggling into her raincoat.

Keith sighed.

How could he plan his new life if he didn't know where his new life was going to be?

"Could be from the Caribbean," said Mrs. Lambert, buttoning up her coat. "Though I'm guessing. I didn't get to eat any fish when I was there. Upset tummy."

Keith's arms were hurting from holding the plastic bag open. He tried to jog her memory.

"Africa?"

Mrs. Lambert looked at him quizzically.

"That's right. I had an upset tummy there, too. How did you know?"

Keith sighed.

• • •

The travel agent wasn't much help either.

"Tropical," he said, "definitely tropical."

He turned to his other customer, a woman in a dripping mac looking glumly through a pile of brochures.

"How about Greece again?" said the travel agent brightly.

The customer shook her head. "The chips tasted of garlic."

Great, thought Keith. Here am I trying to find out about my destiny and he's more worried about a week in Cairo or whatever the capital of Greece is.

"Spain?" said the travel agent. "You liked Spain."

The customer shook her head. "Mum had her shopping trolley nicked."

"Yugoslavia?"

"Palm trees were nylon."

The customer peered into Keith's plastic bag at the fish.

"That's nice," she said. "I like that."

She turned back to the travel agent.

"Where does that come from?" she asked.

"Greece," said the travel agent, avoiding Keith's eyes.

Keith sighed.

• • •

The tropical fish expert at the Natural History Museum was a lot more help.

"Parrot fish," he said. "Found in the tropical north along the Great Barrier Reef."

"Thanks," said Keith.

"Anything else?" said the tropical fish expert.

"Yes," said Keith. "Where's the Great Barrier Reef?"

• • •

Keith stood looking up at the big old stone building. City traffic roared all around it. Pigeons perched high on its grimy windowsills.

For a moment he thought he'd come to the wrong place. Then he saw the sign.

Australia House.

When the man at the museum had told him about Australia House, Keith had imagined a blond brick bungalow with a barbecue and a swimming pool like in "Neighbours."

Oh well, he thought, they probably couldn't get planning permission to build one like that in London.

He went in through the big doors.

The receptionist took a look inside the plastic bag and before Keith could ask her anything, she was talking into her phone.

"Carol," she said, "come and have a look at this."

A woman with hair just like a couple of the women in "Neighbours" came out of a side door and looked into the bag.

"Don't see many of those here in Pommyland," she said.

Keith explained about the hotel and the market and the museum.

"This Great Barrier Reef," he said finally, "is it anywhere near Ramsay Street?"

The receptionist and the woman grinned at each other.

Nice, thought Keith. Instead of grinning like a couple of loonies, how about lending me an Australian street directory?

"Come in here," said the woman.

She led Keith into an office. On the wall was a map of Australia. The woman pointed to a place called Melbourne right down the bottom.

"Ramsay Street, legend has it, is here," she said. "The Great Barrier Reef is up here." She ran her finger along the coastline at the top right-hand corner of Australia.

"Is it a happy sort of place?" asked Keith.

The woman grinned again. "It's underwater," she said, "but apart from that it's pretty happy."

She pointed to a poster further along the wall.

"Here's your bloke, here."

Along the top of the poster it said, "Fish of the Great Barrier Reef." The woman was pointing to a fish just like the one in Keith's bag.

Keith stared.

There were hundreds of them. Hundreds of multicolored fish. All different. All with different names. He imagined Mum and Dad's faces, seeing this. Then he remembered he wasn't trying to cheer them up anymore.

"Beautiful, aren't they?" said the woman. "Beaches up that way aren't too bad either."

She pointed to another poster behind Keith.

He turned around.

It was like a dream, except that Keith's dreams were mostly like the telly with the color knob turned up too high.

This was perfect.

A deserted beach of white sand with palm trees hanging over it and a turquoise sea lapping at the edge. And the bluest sky he'd ever seen.

The only sign of human habitation was a wooden sign on a post in the shade of one of the palm trees.

Keith couldn't read what the sign said, but he knew anyway.

No Misery Guts.

He realized he'd been gazing at the poster for ages and the woman was looking at him.

Never mind. She'd understand when he explained to her that he'd just found the place where he was going to spend the rest of his life.

• • •

All the way home on the train Keith saw nothing but the beach.

Waterloo Bridge, the Bermondsey Gas Works, the Deptford tower blocks, and several thousand gallons of dirty rain slid past the carriage window and Keith missed them all.

He was working out how long till he could get away.

Dennis Baldwin's older brother had left home when he was fourteen. Though that had been to go to a juvenile correction center.

The train pulled into Keith's station and he realized with a shock where he was.

He opened the plastic bag and looked at the fish. "Thanks," he said.

Then he left the fish on the seat so that someone else could find it and have their life changed as well.

• • •

Mum was writing something at the kitchen table when he got in.

She looked up.

"Keith," she said, "here a minute."

Keith's stomach sank. School must have rung up about him being away for the afternoon.

"Love," she said, "about the other night. Dad and me hadn't had a fight. He was on the settee because his tummy was playing up and he kept fidgeting and keeping me awake."

Despite the fact that he wasn't meant to be giving a toss about Dad anymore, Keith felt a twinge of concern.

"Not an ulcer?" he said.

"No," said Mum. "Your cake."

Keith wasn't sure whether to feel relieved or offended.

"Well, partly your cake," Mum continued. "He hasn't been sleeping well for a few months."

She sighed and Keith tried to count the frown lines on her forehead. He got lost at eleven.

"Things are getting him down," she said.

Another entry, thought Keith, for The Most Incredibly Obvious Statement Ever Made.

"What have you got there?" asked Mum.

Keith realized the bundle of Australia House brochures he'd been holding under his jacket had slipped and a couple had fallen onto the floor.

Mum picked one up. She looked at it. "Escape to Queensland's Tropical Far North," it said.

"Are you doing a project on Australia at school?"

Keith was about to say yes, then stopped himself. This was his new life. He didn't want to lie about it.

He didn't say anything.

Mum was looking at the brochure wistfully.

"Looks like paradise," she said. "That's what we could do with, a bit of that."

Keith realized his heart was beating fast.

Mum handed him the brochure.

"Dreams," she said, mostly to herself. She went back to her writing.

Later, in his room, a thought came to him. That was the first time he'd ever seen Mum doing the pools.

• • •

Keith crouched on the stairs and watched Dad at the fryers, skimming golden lumps of cod and rock salmon out of the foaming oil and sliding them into the heated cabinet.

He'd always liked watching Dad fry. Dad always looked good over the fryers, even when he was a bit grumpy. The cabinet lights made his face shine and the steam made his hair curl at the front.

Tonight, though, Keith wasn't looking at the shining cheeks or the curly hair. He was looking at the droopy mouth lines and the dark patches under Dad's eyes.

I can't do it, he thought.

I can't leave them here to plod through a life of sleepless nights and cheap flour and freezing rain and Owen the milkman.

Every time I lie back on that white sand and take a sip from a coconut and let the warm sea breezes clear up a pimple, I'll be thinking of them back here, being misery guts.

Dad lowered a basket of chips into the fryer and the oil bubbled noisily. He stood watching it, shoulders stooped.

I'll have to take them with me, thought Keith.

The thought made something bubble up inside him. Fear, excitement, indigestion, he wasn't sure.

"Dad," he said as casually as he could, strolling into the shop.

Dad looked up.

"Have you ever thought of . . . um . . . moving?"

"Where?" said Dad.

"Um . . . down south. Quite a long way down south."

"What," said Dad, "Lewisham?" He thought about it and shrugged. "No point."

"Further south than that," said Keith. "Australia."

Dad looked at him, taken aback.

"Australia?"

Keith nodded.

Dad suddenly swung around and started frantically scooping pieces of plaice out of the oil. Keith saw they were a bit burned.

Dad turned back to him, mouth almost drooping to the floor.

"I can't even cook fish properly here anymore. Why would I want to go to Australia?"

Chapter Six

K eith pressed the button on the slide projector. Click.

Grandpa appeared on the wall, asleep in a deck chair on a pebble beach under a gray sky.

"Didn't rain the whole week we were away," said Nan to Mum, who was sitting next to her on the settee.

Keith shone his flashlight onto the projector. Only four slides left.

I'll have to do it soon, he thought. His tummy gave a quiver.

"It was windy, mind," Nan continued, "but it didn't rain once."

"Yes, it did," growled Grandpa. "Rained the Thursday night. Twice."

"No, it didn't," said Nan. "That was wind."

Keith heard Dad give a long sort of sigh from the back of the room.

Nan turned to Mum again. "You lot should think about getting away, Marge. You haven't been away for years."

"I know we haven't," said Mum wearily. "Trouble is, holidays aren't easy, what with the shop and everything. Still . . ."

"Next slide, Keith," said Dad.

Keith took a deep breath.

Okay, he thought, this is it. Ten nine eight seven six five four three two one.

Click.

On the wall appeared a gleaming stretch of white sand. An expanse of sparkling turquoise sea. Palm trees against a clear blue sky.

Nice one, thought Keith. Worth every penny of the return trip to Australia House and the ninety potatoes for the slide.

"Blimey," said Nan. "That's not Worthing."

"Bognor," said Grandpa. "That's Bognor, that is."

"Chemist must have mixed them up," said Nan. She peered at the screen. "Doesn't look like Bognor."

Keith fumbled in the dark for his cassette player. He pressed the play button. The sound of a gentle surf filled the room.

At least that's what Keith hoped the others would

think it was. Rather than the sound of an RV 106 steam locomotive climbing a hill just outside Swansea, which had been the closest thing to a gentle surf on Rami Smith's dad's sound-effects record.

"What's that noise?" said Grandpa. "Is there a gas leak?"

"Keith," said Mum, "what's going on?"

Keith switched on the flashlight and shone it on the brochure in his other hand. He started reading in a loud and what he hoped was persuasive voice.

"Tropical Australia, idyllic paradise where your troubles and cares are as far away as yesterday . . ."

"Keith," said Dad. He didn't sound as though his troubles and cares were as far away as yesterday.

Keith pressed on. ". . . where warm, fragrant breezes murmur songs of happiness . . ."

He pulled a can of air freshener from his pocket and sprayed some in the general direction of the others.

". . . and where rainbow choirs of exotic birds proclaim the joys tomorrow holds in store."

He put down the flashlight, the brochure, and the air freshener, cupped his hands to his mouth, and made what he hoped was the happy sound of an exotic tropical bird. Mr. Smith's record had only had ducks.

In the darkness Keith could just make out Mum and Dad and Nan and Granddad staring at him, open-mouthed.

It's working, he thought, they're stunned by the beauty of the place.

He saw they were all frowning.

They're thinking, he told himself, thinking why didn't they go there years ago.

Dad snapped the light on.

"Keith," he said quietly, "I said I didn't want to hear another word about Australia."

"Australia?" said Nan.

"It's all right, Mum," said Mum.

Keith decided to swing his emergency plan into operation. He thrust his hand down behind the armchair cushion and pulled out the soft pink-and-gold fruit that had cost him a hundred and sixty potatoes at Selfridges.

He put it on the coffee table in front of them all.

"The mango," he said, "just part of nature's bounty in Australia's tropical wonderland . . ."

"Keith . . . ," said Dad.

"Keith . . . ," said Mum.

"We'll be able to have fresh ones for breakfast every day," said Keith.

Nan gripped Mum's arm in alarm. "Marge, what's all this about Australia? You're not . . . ?"

"Australia?" said Grandpa. "Nobody said anything to me about Australia."

"There's no way you'd get us going to a place like that," said Nan. "Mrs. Bridge's daughter went. They don't even have corned beef in tins."

48

"Mum . . . ," said Mum.

"Typical," said Grandpa, "nobody ever tells me anything."

"There's nothing to tell," said Dad.

"Mangoes grow on trees out there," said Keith. "They just fall onto the streets. Knee-deep sometimes . . ."

"KEITH," roared Dad, "BE QUIET."

The whole room went quiet.

"We are not," said Dad, almost whispering, "going to Australia."

• • •

Keith lay in bed with his eyes closed, trying to remember.

It was his favorite memory, the one of him when he was a little kid, three or something. He was in a park, watching an ant with wings climb up a dandelion. Next to him on the grass Mum and Dad were talking and laughing softly to each other. Then they went quiet. He looked up at them. They were both gazing at him, smiling gently, eyes shining.

Keith squeezed his eyes shut tighter, trying to see the memory more clearly.

Lately, each time he'd tried, the memory had been getting blurrier and blurrier.

Now, as Keith pushed his fists into his eyelids, he couldn't even see the kid's face.

Perhaps it wasn't even him.

• • •

Keith dusted the pieces of mango with flour and slid them through the bowl of creamy batter and dropped them into the bubbling fat.

Then he opened a tin and did the same with some pineapple rings.

When they'd all turned golden brown he scooped them out with the spatula and put them onto a plate.

He blew hard onto a piece of mango for a couple of minutes, then put it into his mouth.

Mmmm. Nice one. A bit fishy, but otherwise delicious.

He heard footsteps on the stairs and Mum came into the shop.

"I thought I could smell frying," she said sleepily. "Keith, what are you doing? It's Sunday."

"Making breakfast," said Keith. "A typical Australian breakfast."

Mum's shoulders sagged. Then she stared at Keith.

"What have you done to your shirt?"

"It's tropical," said Keith.

Mum closed her eyes.

All right, thought Keith, it's not the most perfect tropical shirt in London, but it's not bad for a first effort.

Next time he'd have to use a tape measure when

he cut the sleeves short so they ended up the same length. And he'd have to learn to paint tropical birds a bit better, too.

Mum opened her eyes.

"Why's it got socks on it?"

"They're parrots."

Mum took a deep breath.

"Don't let Dad see it, Keith. After last night, he's liable to do something drastic."

"I just want us all to be happy," said Keith. "We'd be happy in Australia, I know we would."

Mum looked at him for a long time.

Finally she spoke. "I want us to be happy too, love, and I'd go to Timbuktoo if I thought it'd make any difference."

She looked around the empty shop and out into the overcast street.

"But this is our life and we've just got to make the best of it. Now get that shirt off before Dad gets up."

"What shirt?" said Dad, coming into the shop in his dressing gown.

He stopped and stared at Keith's shirt.

Keith saw his forehead clench into angry ripples. Even more than Mum could get on hers.

Dad opened his mouth to speak.

Keith opened his mouth to speak.

Mum beat them both to it.

"I know," she said, "let's have a day at the sea-side. We haven't been to the seaside in years. Let's have a day at Worthing."

• • •

Keith sat on a deck chair, freezing.

He looked at Mum, sitting on her deck chair, coat buttoned up and scarf wrapped around her throat, doing some knitting. He could tell she was purposely not looking at him.

He looked at Dad, sitting in his deck chair, coat buttoned up, reading the paper. Dad was purposely not looking at him too.

Keith shivered and wished he'd left the sleeves on his tropical shirt. He pulled his jacket tighter around him and wondered if the numbness in his arms was nervous tension or frostbite.

He looked at Mum again.

She smiled at him. He knew it wasn't a real smile. It was the halfhearted lip-stretch people do on windy beaches on overcast days when they want to pretend they're having fun.

Keith looked out across the pebbles. This is ridic-ulous, he thought. Two hours we've been here and neither of them has asked me why I've got a white nose.

He touched his nose to make sure the white coat-ing was still on it.

Yep.

Ask me, thought Keith, ask me.

Because then he could tell them.

"It's the zinc cream people wear in Australia to protect their noses from the sun that shines all day, every day, three hundred and sixty-five days of the year."

And then they'd have to ask themselves why they were freezing to death on Worthing beach when they could be lying under palm trees in North Queensland.

Keith hoped they couldn't tell it was really toothpaste.

He sent a double-strength telepathic message to Mum.

Ask me.

Mum closed her eyes and looked as though she was dropping off to sleep.

Keith sighed and decided to get the fifty pence back he'd paid Dennis Baldwin to teach him the secret of telepathy. Then Dad suddenly screwed up his newspaper and jumped to his feet.

Blimey, thought Keith, my aim must have been crooked.

But Dad didn't mention white noses or white sandy beaches.

"Okay, that's it," he shouted into the wind. "Enough. Finish. We're going home."

53

He started stuffing the thermos and blankets into the picnic bag. Mum opened her eyes, went to say something, then changed her mind.

"We can't go yet," said Keith. "I've only just put my zinc cream on."

Dad came over to Keith and grabbed him by the arm. It hurt.

At least I haven't got frostbite, thought Keith.

"I'm only going to say this once more," said Dad, "so listen very carefully. We are not ever, under any circumstances, going to Australia."

•   •   •

Nobody spoke on the drive back to London.

Keith sat in the back of the van and stared out into the dusk and tried not to feel sad about going to Australia by himself and leaving Mum and Dad behind and probably never seeing them again.

Why should I feel sad, he thought.

It's their fault.

I tried.

He felt his eyes getting hot and prickly.

See, he thought, it's happening already. I'm turning into a misery guts.

He took his mind off things by working out how many potatoes it would take for him to save up the plane fare.

Twenty-five thousand.

He'd better start tomorrow.

Then he closed his eyes and thought about warm white sand and warm turquoise lagoons and glorious pink tropical sunsets.

He opened his eyes just as the van was turning into his street and for a moment he thought he could see one.

A glorious pink tropical sunset.

Then he realized what it was.

A fire.

Blimey, he thought, one of the buildings on our street's on fire.

Suddenly the van was surrounded by red flashing lights and screaming sirens and men running with hoses.

"Whose place is it?" said Mum.

"Can't see," said Dad.

The van moved slowly forward and Keith tried to see whose place it was.

Then he remembered.

The fryer.

The one he'd cooked breakfast in.

He'd forgotten to switch it off.

Chapter Seven

Keith stood in his street at dawn, looking at the sooty wall with the black holes that used to be his life.

The black hole that used to be the kitchen.

The black hole that used to be his bedroom.

The black hole that used to be the shop.

He looked at the edges of the shop hole to see if there was a tiny bit of Tropical Mango that might cheer him up a bit.

Nothing.

Just charred wood and a yellow plastic strip that the fireman had tied across the shop to stop people going in and pinching stuff.

Not that there was anything left to pinch.

Keith realized Mitch Wilson was standing next to

him with a bikeload of newspapers, staring at the black holes. After a bit Mitch pulled their paper from his bag, folded it up, handed it to Dad, and hurried off, his bike wheels crunching over the glass that used to be the shop window.

Mum started sobbing and Dad put his arm around her.

Owen's milk truck pulled up with a whine. Owen stared at the black holes.

"What happened?" he asked.

Nobody answered.

Keith realized he was the one who should speak.

"I burned it down," he said.

• • •

So this is what it feels like to be a misery guts, thought Keith.

He had a vision of spending the rest of his life doing what he'd been doing for most of the day. Lying on cousin Bradley's bed in Auntie Joyce's old bathrobe feeling like there was a black hole inside him bigger than any of the ones he'd seen that morning.

The intergalactic gladiators on the posters around Bradley s bedroom wall glared down at him. Keith knew what they were thinking.

Misery guts.

He stood up.

Okay, he thought. The only way I'm going to get

out of turning into a misery guts is to think positive.

He picked up all his clothes and laid them out carefully on the bed.

Jacket, scarf, tropical shirt, singlet, jeans, socks, underpants, shoes.

He emptied out the pockets of his jacket and jeans and laid those things out too.

Penknife, eighty-four pence, hanky, potato peeler, slide of tropical beach, school bus pass, half a stick of Worthing rock, tube of toothpaste.

Could be worse, he thought. Plenty of kids in the world haven't even got this much. Plenty of kids in the world, if they lost everything in a fire it'd be a pair of shorts, a T-shirt, and a plastic bowl, not a desk with two drawers and a cassette player with detachable speakers and a collection of Green Shield stamps that only needed another 8,940 books for the Ford Escort and a leather football and a book about mountain climbers and a life membership to the Ronnie Barker fan club and a . . .

Stop it.

Think positive.

Mum and Dad still had the clothes they were wearing and there was the van and the picnic basket and the thermos and the deck chairs.

What more did they need to drive to Australia?

He could hear Dad and Uncle Derek downstairs talking to the man from the insurance company.

Surely the insurance money would be enough to pay for the ferry rides over the sea bits.

I've got a choice, thought Keith.

I can go downstairs and tell Mum and Dad how sorry I am and we can all sit around being miserable.

Or I can go down and make it up to them by persuading them to come to Australia where they'll be happy for ever and ever.

It wasn't even a choice, really.

• • •

"Insurance," Uncle Derek was saying, shaking his head, "you pay through the nose, then when it's their turn it's a different story."

The leather armchair Dad was sitting in groaned.

Keith was shocked by how droopy Dad's mouth was. Have to go carefully in Australia, he thought. Too much grinning too quickly and Dad could strain something.

"They're being fair," Dad was saying, "none of the shop equipment was new, or our furniture and clothes and stuff, so you can't expect them to pay the cost of buying new stuff."

The room fell silent.

None of them had seen Keith standing in the doorway. He hitched up his bathrobe.

This was his chance.

He ran through in his head the speech he'd prepared about how it didn't matter so much about being poor if you were happy.

He was about to start saying it when he noticed Mum's eyes. The rims were bright red. She must have been crying for hours.

Suddenly the words Keith had planned to say were scrambled up in his head.

"Will you have enough to open a new shop?" asked Auntie Joyce as she sat down on the settee next to Mum.

The settee groaned.

"Don't know," said Dad.

Keith stopped trying to remember his first speech and rehearsed the second one, the one about how it was cheaper to open up fish-and-chip shops near tropical beaches because you didn't have to spend anything on heating and you could get free salt off the rocks.

He was about to start saying it when Dad sighed.

It was the saddest sigh Keith had ever heard.

He had a vision of them all turning to him after he'd said his speech and just looking at him with long faces and Dad doing another one of those sighs.

He didn't speak.

Uncle Derek sat back in his chair and crossed his legs. The chair groaned.

"Come and work for me," he said to Dad. "Roof insulation's a growth industry. Big opportunities. Okay, you'll have to hoof it around the country with a salesman's bag at first, but after a few years, who knows? I'm thinking of expanding into remote-control garage doors." His face fell. "That's if I can find one that actually works."

"Thanks, Derek," said Dad in a flat voice. "I'll, er . . . I'll think about it."

Keith frantically tried to remember his final speech, the one about the nine hundred and thirty-seven varieties of tropical fish on the Great Barrier Reef.

"You can stay with us as long as you like," said Auntie Joyce. "We've got the spare room and Bradley doesn't mind sharing with Keith."

Bradley, hunched in front of the TV, turned and glared at Keith.

Is it nine hundred and thirty-seven, thought Keith desperately, or nine hundred and seventy-three?

"Thanks, Joyce," said Mum, "but we couldn't."

"Don't worry about the financial side," said Auntie Joyce, "you can make it up to us in baby-sitting. You'd like that, wouldn't you, Diana?"

Diana, lying on the floor picking the plastic veneer off her Walkman, looked up at Mum.

"Our last baby-sitter," she said, "cut her head open on the microwave."

Nearly a thousand, thought Keith, that'll do.

He opened his mouth to speak.

But Mum and Dad, sitting there, looked so unhappy that Keith couldn't get the words out.

When people were that unhappy it just seemed wrong to try and cheer them up.

Keith had never felt that before in his life but he did now.

And with an awful feeling of dread, he realized what it meant.

It's happened, he thought. I've become a misery guts.

• • •

In bed that night he tried everything he could think of to cheer himself up.

Jokes, Ronnie Barker TV sketches he knew by heart, a replay of the time the school team beat Kidbrooke six-nil, memories of when Eric Cox's mum worked in a chocolate frog factory and she was allowed to bring home the ones without legs.

No good.

He was a misery guts.

As he finally drifted off to sleep, he was half aware of Mum and Dad coming into the room.

They must be sick of all the roof insulation stacked in the spare room, he thought sleepily and rolled over in bed to make space for them.

"Keith," said Dad, "are you awake?"

Keith struggled awake.

Bradley was snoring on the blow-up bed on the floor.

Mum and Dad led Keith to the spare room. They

sat him on the bed and stood over him. Keith could see piles of roof insulation looming up behind them.

"Fourteen years we kept that shop going," said Dad, "and now it's finished."

Here it comes, thought Keith sadly. The accusations. The blame.

"I'm sorry, Dad," he said.

"Half a million pieces of fish we sold," said Dad.

"I'm sorry."

"Twenty-five million chips. Two hundred thousand pickled onions. A hundred thousand bags of peas. And now I'm faced with spending the rest of my life selling roof insulation."

"Dad," said Keith miserably, "I'm sorry. I forgot about the fryer. It's my fault."

"Keith," said Mum, "Dad and I have made a decision."

Here it comes, thought Keith. The punishment.

What would it be? Making him leave school to get a job to pay them back? A juvenile correction center?

"We've decided," said Dad, "to go to Australia."

Chapter Eight

On the plane to Istanbul, Keith wrote a postcard.

Dear Uncle Derek and Auntie Joyce,
  Please thank your friend the travel agent for fixing up the cheap tickets. When Dad found out how much the full-price ones were I thought he was going to change his mind. I could tell from your faces you thought he was too. Love to Bradley and Diana, and Mum hopes Bradley's rash from the blow-up bed has cleared up.
  Love, Keith.

At Istanbul Airport he wrote another.

Dear Nan and Grandpa,

Thanks for the tropical shirt. I'm saving it to wear when we land in Australia. I'll also wear it when we've got rich and you come out for a visit. Nan, I've checked up and you can't get cholera or typhoid in Australia, or Yangzte Fever, so don't worry. Mum and Dad are well, but Dad is in a bit of a bad mood. He says seven and a half hours is too long to wait between planes. I think he just can't wait to get to Australia.

Love, Keith.

He wrote two more on the plane to Karachi.

Dear Mr. Naylor,

Mum asked me to drop you a line to say thanks for having us to tea last Tuesday and she's very glad the fire didn't damage your wallpaper. It's a small world. Dad is sitting next to a German salesman who sells wallpaper. He's been telling Dad all about it for over three hours.

Your ex-neighbor, Keith Shipley.

P.S. Thankfully you were wrong about taking off in planes. We've done it twice now and none of our eardrums have exploded.

Dear Owen,

Please cancel all milk deliveries to our place, if you haven't already.

Yours sincerely, Keith Shipley.

And another two at Karachi Airport.

Dear Mrs. Lambert,

Guess what? We're in Pakistan and we've got upset tummies too. I reckon it's the sandwiches we bought when they said our next flight was delayed ten hours. Was the plane delayed on your trip to Africa? Please tell the class they're very welcome to visit us in Australia at any time and that goes for you too but I'd stick to biscuits at the airports.

Yours faithfully, Keith Shipley, Indian subcontinent.

Dear Mr. Crouch,

I've just been talking to a cleaner who used to live in Bristol till he was deported and he says they're short of good science teachers here in Pakistan. Bear in mind that the language might be a problem. Dad spent ten minutes trying to tell the guard at the security gate he was only going to Australia 'cause Mum wanted to. The guard thought he was talking about radial tyres.

Your ex-student, K. Shipley.

P.S. I'm sure Dad was only joking.

On the plane to Colombo, he wrote another.

Dear Dennis,

My parents have stopped talking to each other just like yours did on holiday in Dorset. They haven't hit each other with any chairs yet though. This is because they know Australia will be wonderful once we get there. Tell Sally Prescott that in Australia all mums and dads are happy.

Keith.

And another on the plane to Jakarta.

Dear Rami,

All the airports we've been to on this trip have had armed soldiers guarding them. I think this is to stop all the local people crowding onto the planes to get to Australia. Sorry I didn't hang around the other day but it's very hard saying good-bye to people who are in the middle of kicking the seats out of a bus shelter.

Keith.

He wrote the last one on the plane to Cairns.

Dear Uncle Derek and Auntie Joyce,

Please tell your friend the travel agent that five different airlines is a bit too much for older people. I'm fine, but 73 hours is a long trip when you're over 30.

I'm sure Mum and Dad would send their love if they were awake.

Love, Keith.

Then the pilot announced that they had just commenced flying over the continent of Australia.

Keith forgot his stomach, which felt like a knotted hosepipe. He forgot his mouth, which felt like a bath that hadn't been wiped out for months. He forgot his eyes, which felt like tinned peaches in bowls of cornflakes.

Australia.

He peered out the window.

Far below he could see browns and greens and the flash of sun on water.

He turned to Mum and Dad, to shake them and hug them and let them see for themselves. But their sleeping faces looked so exhausted he decided not to wake them up.

Plenty of time for grinning and hugging each other when they were on the ground.

At Orchid Cove.

For about the ten-thousandth time since the woman at Australia House had told him what the tropical beach on her wall was called, Keith said the words quietly to himself.

Orchid Cove.

He had a sudden urge to do some cartwheels up the aisle of the plane.

Instead he went into one of the plane toilets and changed into Nan and Grandpa's tropical shirt. It was green and purple with scenes of tourist attractions in Hawaii on it.

Who cares, thought Keith happily. It's tropical. He smeared some toothpaste on his nose.

As he walked back to his seat he noticed that for the first time some of the other passengers were smiling.

He smiled back.

Australia, he thought. What other country could cheer up a planeload of misery guts at sixty thousand feet?

• • •

Keith didn't notice the heat until they were on the airport bus into Cairns.

He was staring out the window, marveling at how bright the shops and houses were even though he was wearing the sunglasses he'd bought in Lewisham.

"I think," said Dad, "we should try and find a shop here in Cairns."

Keith's stomach gave a lurch. Cairns looked like a nice place, much cleaner and brighter than London, but he'd only counted four palm trees since they'd left the airport and the only stretch of sand he'd seen was in a builder's yard. And Orchid Cove was only one more bus ride away.

"Dad," he said desperately, "look at all the fish-and-chip shops and hamburger places and pizza parlors and takeaway Chinese restaurants."

As he spoke he prayed they'd pass some. They did, a row of shops with at least one of each.

"Keith's right, love," said Mum. "Let's go and have a look at Orchid Cove."

The bus turned a corner and they passed another fish-and-chip shop.

"All right," said Dad.

Keith's pulse slowed down. He realized he was dripping with sweat.

And the bus was air-conditioned.

• • •

The bus to Orchid Cove wasn't air-conditioned.

Keith decided it was like sitting in a warm bath that was over your head but you could still breathe.

He liked it.

But it did make you feel very sleepy.

He watched the suburbs of Cairns slipping past the window, then fields of green stuff that were higher than the bus. Giant shallots, he thought sleepily.

He had a vision of an Australian salad. Lettuce leaves as big as bedspreads. Tomatoes as big as bubble cars. Cucumbers as big as tube trains.

Then someone was shaking his shoulder.

Keith opened his eyes.

70

It was Mum.

The light outside the bus had changed. It wasn't bright anymore, it was dull, but glowing at the same time.

Keith staggered off the bus behind Mum and Dad. The bus driver dragged their suitcases out of the luggage compartment, climbed back in, and the bus roared away down the narrow road.

Keith saw why the light was different. The sky was glowing with pink and gold and purple and a color that made his tired eyes open wide.

Tropical Mango.

Across the road, tall and dark against the sunset, a row of slender trunks hung over a sandy beach, fronds gently swaying.

Palm trees.

Keith walked slowly over and stood under the palm trees on the warm sand and watched the waves breaking, pink and frothy like the strawberry milkshake he'd had a couple of hours earlier.

A warm breeze blew against his face. He took a deep breath and smelled more wonderful tropical smells than he'd ever smelled before. Even including the time Bradley dropped the iron onto Auntie Joyce's bottles of perfume.

Keith felt two arms slide around his shoulders. He looked up. Mum and Dad were standing close to him, their faces aglow with huge smiles.

Paradise.

Chapter Nine

Keith opened his eyes and didn't know where he was.

Above his head was a curved metal ceiling with rivets in it.

Then he remembered.

Van Number Six, Orchid Cove Caravan Park, Orchid Cove, Paradise.

Over in the other bed Mum and Dad were still asleep. Keith looked at his watch. Six-thirty Australian time. He pulled the curtain aside. Sunlight spilled onto his bed.

Fantastic, he thought.

He lay back for a bit and just enjoyed having sunlight on his bed at six-thirty in the morning. Then he got down to business.

Okay. Plan for the day. Explore paradise, then when Mum and Dad wake up, take them on the grand tour.

Nice one.

He slipped out of bed and put on his tropical shirt and his new shorts, the ones Mum had made him on Auntie Joyce's Swedish sewing machine. He put his shoes on with no socks. Then he put some toothpaste on his nose and stepped quietly out of the caravan.

The air was clean and warm and smelled like air freshener, only much better.

In the lush green forest at the back of the caravan park Keith could see flashes of color as red and blue birds swooped among the trees. They looked like West Ham practicing diving headers.

He walked to the beach. It was even better than the night before.

In the morning sun the sand was a brilliant white and the sea was a sparkling turquoise. The sky was a deep blue and the fronds of the palm trees shone emerald green.

Perfect, thought Keith. Just like the poster in Australia House.

Except for the girl fishing.

He stood and watched as the girl down near the water's edge swung her big rod and cast her line out over the waves.

I wonder if fishing's easy to learn, he thought.

73

Be handy, me popping down here before breakfast each morning and catching all the fish for the shop.

She didn't look any older than him.

He went closer for a better look, down onto the wet sand where the girl was standing.

She turned and stared at him. Her eyes were almost as pale as her hair and her face was very brown.

Keith noticed pink patches where the brown was peeling off her nose and wondered if he should offer her some toothpaste.

He decided not to.

"Hello, I'm Keith."

"G'day, I'm Tracy."

"Caught anything?"

"Bit of a cough last winter. Better now but."

She grinned at him.

Keith grinned back. Here they were, only met two seconds ago and she was cracking jokes already. What a place.

The water looked cool and tempting. Keith kicked off his shoes and stepped in up to his ankles.

"Wouldn't if I was you," said Tracy.

"Why not?" said Keith.

"Stingers."

Keith looked at her blankly.

Stingers?

"Sea wasps," said Tracy.

Sea wasps?

Keith knew all about wasps, he'd had plenty attack his jam sandwiches on picnics, and he knew they couldn't live underwater because he and Dennis Baldwin had tried to teach one to swim once. Must be another joke.

"Box jellyfish," said Tracy slowly and more loudly. She held out a pair of green tights to Keith. "Put these on if you want to go for a paddle. Won't stop them stinging you but at least the buggers won't kill you."

Kill?

Keith stepped quickly out of the water.

Tracy pointed toward the palm trees. "It's got all about 'em over there."

Keith saw Tracy was pointing to a sign on a wooden pole.

Keith recognized it as the sign he hadn't been able to read in the Australia House poster.

He walked into the shade of the palm trees and read the sign. Blimey, he thought, she's right. Box jellyfish. Waters around North Queensland coast. Sting fatal.

Keith felt panic starting in his stomach.

Killer jellyfish?

In paradise?

What would Mum and Dad say when they found out he'd brought them twelve thousand miles on five different airlines to a place with killer jellyfish?

He forced himself to calm down.

Okay, so they wouldn't be able to swim in the sea. No big deal. They could still lie on the white sand under the swaying palm fronds.

He looked at the palm tree he was standing under. Around the base of the fronds, high above him, he saw a cluster of big round greeny-brown things. It took him a moment to work out what they were.

Coconuts.

Suddenly he felt fine again. What were a few killer jellyfish compared to being able to lie back in the shade, drinking from a fresh coconut?

"Wouldn't stay under there too long," yelled Tracy.

Why not? thought Keith.

"Split your skull open if one of 'em falls on you."

Keith looked at the palm tree. It must be a hundred years old, how was it going to fall on him? Then he realized Tracy meant the coconuts.

Keith looked down the beach at her and wondered if she was only nine and big for her age. Nine-year-olds panicked about things like coconuts falling on you.

Tracy was yelling at him again, pointing across the road.

"Look over there."

Keith turned and looked.

Across the road was a high fence and behind it Keith could see the top of what looked like a hotel. Just inside the fence was another row of palm trees.

Two men up ladders were cutting the coconuts off and throwing them down.

Must be the coconut harvest, thought Keith.

"Go and ask them what they're doing," yelled Tracy.

Keith went over, feeling a bit of a wally, but curious.

"What are you doing?" he called up.

"We're missile experts," said one of the men with a grin, "removing dangerous missiles. Bit of a breeze and these mongrels'd drop on your head and crack your skull open."

As he spoke he accidentally knocked one of the coconuts with his arm. It hurtled down and smacked into the road near Keith.

The man looked down, alarmed. "Jeez, sorry," he said. "You'd better shift away a bit."

Keith looked at the coconut at his feet. It wasn't even cracked. Then he saw the dent in the tarmac where the coconut had hit the road.

Killer coconuts and killer jellyfish.

Keith had a sudden urge to run back to the caravan and crawl back into bed and pretend none of this had happened.

Instead he walked back down the beach to Tracy, who he decided was definitely the same age as him.

"Heard one drop," said Tracy. "Thought you'd copped it for a sec."

"Tracy," said Keith, "is there any other dangerous stuff around here?"

Tracy squinted out to sea.

"Not really," she said.

Keith felt relief seep through him.

"There's the stonefish, of course," said Tracy, "but they only kill you if you tread on them. Little buggers lie on the bottom looking like rocks."

Keith looked down to see if he was standing on any rocks.

"And the pufferfish," continued Tracy, "but you've got to actually eat a bit of one before you die."

Think positive, thought Keith.

"What about rivers? Are there any good rivers for swimming in?"

"Some beauties," said Tracy. "The crocs come from miles around to swim in 'em."

Crocs, thought Keith. Must be a local expression for old people.

"Tourist got eaten by a crocodile only last month," said Tracy.

Keith wished he hadn't mentioned rivers.

Then he remembered the forest, cool and green and alive with exotic birds.

"Just as well there's the forest," he said. "Bet it's paradise in there for a picnic."

"Top spot on a hot day," said Tracy. "Cooler than an esky in there."

Keith started to plan the picnic he'd take Mum and Dad on at lunchtime.

"But you wouldn't actually sit down in there," said Tracy. "Mosquitoes'd have their own picnic if you did. Plus there's the poisonous spiders and poisonous snakes. Great spot for a bushwalk but."

Tracy then told Keith the story of her uncle's cousin's brother who'd been bitten by a snake in a phone box near a cane field and who'd been dead before he could ring for an ambulance.

• • •

Keith walked slowly back to the caravan.

"It'll be okay," he said to himself.

It made him feel better so he said it again. A couple of hundred times.

Mum and Dad didn't have to know.

The important thing was to keep them cheerful so they could get a shop going and it could be a big success and they could all be happy.

All I've got to do, he decided, is keep them off the beach, out of rivers, and out of the rain forest.

And away from Tracy.

In the caravan Dad was making toast.

"Did you see Mum on your walk?" he asked.

Keith felt his stomach drop into the familiar bowl of cold batter.

Mum had already gone out.

She probably knew everything by now. At this

very moment she was probably down on the beach listening to Tracy describe how a giant squid had eaten someone's grandfather.

Then Keith had a worse thought.

What if she'd gone for a paddle in a river?

He heard someone coming up the steps.

He couldn't look.

Who would it be? The police? A wheelchair salesman?

He looked.

It was Mum, with a big smile on her face.

"Guess what?" she said. "I've found us a shop."

Chapter Ten

It was the best-looking shop Keith had ever seen.

It was more of a cottage than a shop, with a gleaming galvanized iron roof and fresh cream paint on the wooden walls and colored plastic strips hanging in the doorway.

And it was a good ten yards from the nearest palm tree.

All it needs, thought Keith happily, is a sign on the front.

Paradise Fish Bar.

"Good position," said Mum, pointing to the other shops nearby. "General store, chemist, hardware, swimwear boutique, and cake shop. Good assortment of customers and no direct competition."

Dad looked up and down the dusty main street of Orchid Cove, then over the road at the beach.

For an awful moment Keith thought Dad had heard about the jellyfish.

"Should be some trade from the petrol station down on the corner," said Dad.

Keith stopped holding his breath.

See, he said to himself, it's going to be all right.

Mum led them in through the colored plastic strips.

Keith looked around. The shop was dark and cool inside, and empty except for dusty shop fittings. Leaning against a wall were some old posters for something called a Chiko Roll.

"The woman who owns it retired last month," said Mum. "Sold all her stock and put the place up for rent."

"What about equipment?" asked Dad.

"Fridge," said Mum, pointing to a fridge. "Sink," she said, pointing to a sink. She pulled aside a pile of cardboard boxes. "Fryer." she said, pointing to a fryer. She gave Dad a grin. "We're in business. We can open in a week."

Dad looked at her. "What about the paperwork?"

"The place is still registered as a takeaway food shop," said Mum. "Mrs. McIntyre is happy for us to leave things as they are for now and when the renewal comes up we can change it over then."

Dad looked doubtful.

"Look," said Mum, "if we're going to make a new life here, there's going to be lots of paperwork to sort out later on. First we've got to make the shop a success, right?"

"Right," said Keith loudly.

Mum smiled and slipped her arm around Keith and gave him a squeeze.

They both looked at Dad, who was staring at the fryer with a gloomy face.

"Probably hasn't been serviced for ten years," he said.

Don't think about that stuff, thought Keith. *Don't.* He'd given up telepathy but this was an emergency.

Mum grabbed Dad and turned him toward the window.

"Look," she said, pointing across the road at the sea sparkling through the palm fronds. "Does this look like the sort of place where fryers break down?"

Dad stared at the sea for a good minute.

If a jellyfish jumps out of the water now we've had it, thought Keith.

Then Dad turned back to them and rubbed his hands together.

"Let's get started," he said. "We've got a big job ahead of us."

You're not kidding, thought Keith.

He hadn't checked under the shop for snakes yet.

* * *

While Mum started cleaning up the shop and Dad got on the phone to Cairns to order oil and potatoes and matzo flour, Keith checked under the shop for snakes.

The shop was built on wooden stumps, which meant he could walk around under it if he crouched low enough. It also meant he had room to swing the old machete he found hanging on one of the stumps.

He had to do that twice.

The first time was when he put his foot on a thirty-foot diamond-bellied black snake which he chopped into eight pieces before he saw the metal nozzle that connected it to the garden tap.

The second time was when he backed into a crocodile.

He felt its rough skin scrape the back of his legs.

Heart pounding, he slowly raised the machete, spun around, slipped, and sat down on the crocodile.

The crocodile had arm rests.

What a stupid place to leave an old vinyl settee, thought Keith. He sat back and waited for his heart to calm down.

He could hear Mum and Dad banging around above him with mops and brooms.

At least, he thought, they're too busy to be planning any picnics in the rain forest or paddles at the beach.

He'd still hide their swimming costumes and the picnic plates, just in case.

• • •

The people of Orchid Cove were everything Keith had hoped they would be.

Cheerful.

Ron in the general store was cheerful. Clarrie the chemist was cheerful. Doug at the petrol station was so cheerful you could hear him whistling even when he was taking wheel nuts off with a power tool.

Complete strangers were cheerful. They nodded to each other on the street and said "G'day" and complimented each other on their new hats and cars and, in Keith's case, the new zinc cream on his nose. They said blue was a good choice of color.

Only twice did Keith come across people in Orchid Cove who were not what he had hoped they would be.

The first time was early one morning, before Mum and Dad were awake, while Keith was making his daily circuit of the shower block, bashing the long grass with a stick to scare away snakes. (The caravan park owner had taken his machete away.)

Suddenly, from one of the other caravans, Keith heard two people shouting at each other.

"I'm sick of this and I'm sick of you, you lazy, dirty pig," shouted a woman's voice.

"Yeah, well, if I'm a pig," shouted a man's voice, "it's because this place is a pigsty."

Keith went over and banged on the caravan door. It was opened by a man with a bare chest and a red face.

"Do you mind," said Keith. "There are plenty of big cities for that sort of thing. People have come here to be cheered up."

The man scowled at him and slammed the door.

Later that day Keith spent some of Uncle Derek's going-away money on a bunch of flowers and a bar of chocolate, which he left on the red-faced man's caravan step. It was what Mum and Dad gave each other when they'd been fighting and it seemed to work for them.

The second incident was in the hardware store when Keith was waiting to buy some tile adhesive for Dad.

The old man in front of Keith asked for twelve nails, and a young assistant with pimples and a thin mustache rolled his eyes and made a sarcastic comment about building a new house.

Keith stepped forward.

"If you do anything like that again," he said to the assistant, "I'll report you to the Far North Queensland Tourist Office."

The assistant stared at him, open-mouthed.

"Next time you feel grumpy," said Keith, "go out the back and read this."

He pulled a comic from his back pocket and gave it to the startled assistant.

It was the only comic he'd brought from England, and he knew he was going to miss it, but it was for a good cause.

Chapter Eleven

Opening Today said the banner across the front of the shop.

Keith looked up at the banner proudly. Sixteen sheets of wrapping paper and two rolls of sticky tape and it was holding together perfectly.

He closed his eyes and made a wish.

I wish, he thought, that we get loads of customers and they all buy at least two bits of fish and none of them say anything about relatives who went for a paddle and never came back.

Then he went through the colored plastic strips and stood behind the counter with Mum and Dad.

He could tell they were nervous too.

Mum was going over the potatoes he'd peeled

earlier, checking each one for eyes and bits of missed skin before she cut it into chips.

Keith watched her remove an eye that was so tiny an ant wouldn't have seen it without glasses.

Be fair, he thought, what do you expect for 4.13 cents a potato at the current rate of exchange?

Dad was battering fish more slowly and carefully than Keith had ever seen him do it.

Normally Dad floured and battered with short flicks of the wrist that made Keith wonder why Dad didn't get a table tennis table and have a crack at the world championships. This morning, though, as Dad dragged each piece of fish carefully through the batter, he looked like he was playing the violin.

Keith caught himself having another quick glance at the fish. The vision flashed into his head again. The vision of their customers taking a bite of fish, screwing up their faces and dropping dead in the middle of reaching for the vinegar.

Stop it, he told himself. You're being silly. A fish co-op would not deliver stonefish or pufferfish for public consumption.

Then the plastic strips rattled and a man came into the shop.

Their first customer.

Keith gave him a big We-Don't-Know-You-Yet-But-We-Hope-You'll-Be-A-Regular-Customer smile.

Then Keith realized he did know him.

He felt the smile trickle off his face.

It was Mr. Gambaso from the milk bar at the other end of the street.

And he was holding something behind his back.

Suddenly Keith had another vision. An argument with insults and shouting and hurtful comments about stealing customers and who was here first. Then Mr. Gambaso brandishing the bread knife he was holding behind his back and running amok.

Keith prayed that Mr. Gambaso wouldn't say who he was. That he'd just look around and leave quietly.

"Good morning," said Mr. Gambaso. "I'm Joe Gambaso from the milk bar."

That's it, thought Keith, we're goners.

"Morning," said Dad, "Vin Shipley. What can we do for you?"

"Just dropped in to wish you luck on your first day," said Mr. Gambaso. From behind his back he produced a soggy brown paper bag. "I brought you a hamburger."

He put it on the counter. They all looked at it.

"You, er . . . you don't do hamburgers here, do you?" asked Mr. Gambaso.

"No, we don't," said Dad.

Mr. Gambaso visibly relaxed.

"It's very kind of you," said Mum. "Vin, go on." She pointed to the fryer.

Dad served up a fish-and-chips for Mr. Gambaso.

"You, er . . . you don't do fish-and-chips down

at your place, Joe?" said Dad as he handed them over.

"No," said Mr. Gambaso.

Dad smiled and soon they were all munching away and chatting about cooking oils.

Phew, thought Keith as he watched them, that was a close one.

• • •

Their first real customer came in fifteen minutes later.

It was Doug from the petrol station.

"Morning tea," he said with a big grin.

For a moment Keith thought Doug wanted a cup of tea and some biscuits. He could tell from their faces that Mum and Dad did too.

"If I don't have a decent feed for morning tea I'm cactus by lunch," said Doug with an even bigger grin. "Two bits of fish and a dollar's worth of chips, thanks."

When the order was cooked Dad tipped it into the paper and put in on the counter like he always did so the customer could do their own salt and vinegar.

Doug grabbed the bottle of ketchup that Mr. Gambaso had warned them they should have on the counter and shook big puddles of it all over his fish-and-chips.

Keith stared.

"Vinegar?" asked Dad weakly.

"No, ta," said Doug, "I'm on a diet."

Their next customer was the woman who worked in the chemist's. She introduced herself as Raylene and while her fish was in she told them about Mrs. Newman in the post office's daughter's baby that could hum the theme to "Flying Doctors."

Outside the shop Raylene stopped and ate a couple of mouthfuls and stuck her head back in through the plastic strips.

"Jeez," she said, "you Poms sure know how to make fish-and-chips."

After that it seemed to Keith that most of Orchid Cove came in at some stage during the day. Even the hardware store assistant with the pimples and the thin moustache. He bought four lots of fish-and-chips, one with double salt, and gave Keith a motorbike magazine.

• • •

That evening Keith climbed slowly up the stepladder and took the Opening Today banner down.

His legs were aching but inside he felt like doing several cartwheels and a couple of handstands.

Fifty-three customers, eighty-one pieces of fish, and not one mention of a snake or a sea wasp.

"G'day, Keith."

Keith spun around.

In the dusk Tracy's skin looked browner than it

had on the beach. Against all that brown her grin looked like a toothpaste advert, only crooked. At her feet was a small dog.

"This is Buster," said Tracy. "You didn't say you had a fish-and-chip shop."

"It only opened today," mumbled Keith. He couldn't take his eyes off the dog, which only had three legs and half an ear.

It looked like something had tried to eat it and then spat it out. A crocodile? A jellyfish? A really big spider?

"You should have told me," Tracy was saying. "Mum would have got some for our tea."

Keith mumbled that they were about to close up anyway. He glanced in the window. Mum and Dad were watching them, smiling.

Tracy was hunting through her pockets.

Don't go in and buy anything, please, thought Keith. If you go in they'll ask you about the dog.

"Skint," said Tracy. "Oh well."

"Bye," said Keith.

He started to go into the shop.

"Keith," she said.

He stopped. Go home, he thought, please go home.

"The other morning, when I was telling you about Uncle Wal's cousin's brother who got bitten by the snake in the phone box, I didn't mean to make you feel crook. Sorry."

Crook?

Whatever it meant, he wasn't going to admit to it.

"You didn't," he said.

"Oh, good," she said. "It's just that when I said that bit about him being sick through his nose, I thought you went sorta pale. Dad's always saying I should leave that bit out, but I get carried away."

"I was fine," said Keith, feeling pale all over again.

He glanced in through the window and felt even paler.

Mum and Dad were coming out of the shop.

"Keith," said Dad, "Mum and me have been having a chat. It's been all work and no play since we got here so we've decided to go for a picnic on Saturday. Beach, rain forest, wherever you like."

"And we were wondering," said Mum, smiling at Tracy, "if your friend would like to come too?"

"Yeah," said Tracy, grinning, "I'd like that."

Chapter Twelve

You burned it down?"

Keith sighed.

He'd done that bit about five minutes ago. Some people's powers of concentration were pathetic.

Tracy was staring at him, the scab she'd been picking on her knee totally forgotten. Buster, curled up next to her in the old hammock, was staring at him too.

"I left the fryer on," said Keith, "and that burned it down."

"Jeez," said Tracy, "your parents must have been ropeable."

Keith sighed again. He'd already explained how Mum and Dad had been upset and depressed, and angry if that's what ropeable meant.

"That's the whole point," he said. "They're happy now and they'll stay happy all the while they think this place is paradise."

Tracy had gone back to picking her scab.

Great, thought Keith, here I am pouring out my innermost secrets to an almost complete stranger and she's not even listening.

Tracy's mum came out onto the veranda, the weathered old boards creaking under her brown feet. She was holding two cans of drink.

"Guess what, Mum," said Tracy. "Keith burned their fish-and-chip shop in England down."

Keith sighed.

"I'm sure he didn't mean to," said Tracy's mum, smiling at Keith. "Lemonade or Fanta?"

Keith took the lemonade, thanked Tracy's mum, and wished it was her who was coming on the picnic.

Tracy's mum went back inside.

When the wire screen door had stopped banging, Keith tried to continue.

"That's why I don't want them to know about the jellyfish and crocodiles and snakes and stuff. That's why we've got to find somewhere for the picnic that doesn't have any of those things."

He looked up to see if Tracy understood now.

She wasn't even looking at him. She was watching a dusty car pull up next to the house. A man with hair as fair as hers got out of the car with a fishing rod in sections and a bucket.

"G'day, Dad," said Tracy. "This is Keith. He burned their fish-and-chip shop in England down."

"So," said Tracy's dad, "you're the Poms Trace has been telling us about. G'day."

He held out his hand and Keith shook it.

Something didn't feel right. Keith realized he was only shaking three fingers and a thumb. There was a finger missing.

Perhaps, thought Keith, Tracy's dad and Buster had a fight and Buster bit off Tracy's dad's finger and Tracy's dad bit off Buster's leg and half his ear.

It didn't seem likely.

He tried not to stare at the missing finger.

"If your dad likes fishing," Tracy's dad was saying, "send him round. They're biting real well at the moment."

He showed them the bucket. Inside were three big pink fish.

"Or snorkeling," he went on. "Reef's a knockout if you haven't seen it. Better than telly."

He ruffled Keith's hair and went inside.

Keith looked at Tracy.

"Do you understand about the picnic now?" he asked.

"He scratched it on some coral when he was seventeen," said Tracy. "It got infected and he had to have it chopped off."

Keith took a deep breath.

"We've got to find somewhere for a picnic," he

97

said, "with no crocodiles, no jellyfish, no snakes, and no coral."

• • •

The day of the picnic was very hot.

"So where's this surprise destination?" said Dad, locking up the door of the caravan. "I bet it's the rain forest."

"Stop it," said Mum, wedging his new straw hat onto his head, "it's a surprise. We'll find out when we get there."

Keith grabbed one handle of Mum's shopping bag and waited for Dad to grab the other.

He wished the day was over and he was in bed. No such luck.

Dad grabbed the other handle and they started walking toward the road, sandwiches rustling in greaseproof paper and bottles clinking.

"Have you always lived here, Tracy?" asked Mum.

"I was born here," said Tracy. "Well, not exactly here. We used to live inland a bit, near Crocodile Falls."

Keith felt the blood drain from most of his body.

"Why's it called Crocodile Falls?" asked Dad.

This is it, thought Keith, in two seconds we'll be running back to the caravan.

" 'Cause the rocks at the bottom are so jagged," said Tracy.

Thank God, thought Keith.

"Like teeth," said Tracy.

Enough, thought Keith, don't go on.

He looked up and saw Tracy giving him a little grin.

They were almost at the beach.

"If we're going to the beach," said Dad, "I'll have to go back. I've forgotten my swimming trunks."

"We're not going to the beach," said Keith hastily. "Tracy's got somewhere better."

"It's along here," said Tracy.

They walked along the road, past the shop, and kept on going.

"Hope it's not much further," said Mum. "It's getting a bit hot."

"Nearly there," said Tracy.

Keith had one more go at wishing the day was over and he was in bed.

Still no good.

Tracy led them into the grounds of the Orchid Cove Public School. They walked across the dusty playground and past the white wooden school building.

Behind the school was a playing field, mown into an oval and scorched yellow by the sun. In one corner was a metal climbing frame. Tracy stopped next to it.

"Here we are," she said. "Don't climb on it, you'll burn your hands."

"Isn't it a great spot?" said Keith. He unfolded the tarpaulin Tracy's dad had lent them and heaved it over the top of the climbing frame.

"See," he said, "shade twenty-four hours a day."

He and Tracy crawled inside and started unpacking the picnic things.

Keith risked a glance up at Mum and Dad.

Dad was staring as if he'd never seen a climbing frame with a tarpaulin over it before.

Mum was looking a bit doubtful too. Then suddenly she grinned. And chuckled. And put her arm around Dad.

"They said it'd be a surprise," she laughed. "I'm surprised, are you surprised?"

Dad broke into a grin too. "I'm very surprised," he said.

Keith felt his heart start to slow down. He wondered if all this stress was going to catch up with him later in life.

Mum and Dad crawled in with them under the tarpaulin and they all ate the sandwiches and drank the fizzy drinks while Tracy explained that this was the place where Russell Kinlock in year six had broken the world record for hanging upside down by his legs until a seagull had landed on him and he'd panicked and sprained his pelvis.

Mum and Dad roared with laughter.

Keith was delighted, even though he didn't see

what was so funny. He'd sprained his ankle once and it had hurt like anything.

Then Tracy went out onto the oval and reenacted Orchid Cove Public School winning the Far North Queensland Under Twelves Softball Shield.

She did it all in slow motion and had Mum and Dad in stitches.

Keith realized, as he watched her do a slow-motion diving catch, that he'd never met anyone like her before.

Chapter Thirteen

No more, thanks, Mrs. Shipley," said Tracy, flopping back against the caravan wall, "I'm stuffed."

Keith wasn't surprised.

Six pieces of cheese on toast she'd just had, four of them with tomato. And two pieces of fruitcake.

Mum went to the other end of the caravan to turn the kettle down.

Keith leaned forward across the fold-down table and whispered to Tracy.

"Thanks."

She deserved it. Three hours at the picnic and an hour and a half at the tea table and she hadn't mentioned snakes or jellyfish once.

Keith realized Tracy was giving him a strange look. Probably indigestion.

"Great tea but," Tracy called out to Mum. "Thanks for inviting me back."

"Our pleasure, Tracy," said Mum, "I haven't laughed so much in years."

"Me neither," called Dad from outside. He was sitting on the caravan steps going through the first week's paperwork from the shop.

"What about you, Keith?" asked Mum. "More cake?"

"No thanks," said Keith.

"You've hardly eaten anything," said Mum.

Keith gave Tracy a look which he hoped said, "Parents, couldn't you take them outside and bury them?"

When he thought about it, though, he had to admit Mum was right. He had hardly eaten anything. This must have been partly because he was laughing so much at Tracy's tales of life at Orchid Cove Public School, and partly because his stomach was knotted with excitement.

He had a plan.

It had come to him halfway through Tracy telling them about Mr. Caulfield, a teacher who could do Donald Duck talk with his armpit.

Tracy's parents.

If Tracy could do it, be positive about Orchid Cove

and not mention the bad stuff, perhaps her parents could too. And then Mum and Dad could make friends with them and spend evenings and weekends chatting with them on the veranda and never need to go to the beach or the rain forest.

It was worth a try.

"Mum," said Keith, "you should meet Tracy's parents. They're great, aren't they, Tracy?"

Tracy smiled. "Yeah, they're tops."

"That would be very nice, Tracy," said Mum.

"Yes," said Dad, coming in from the steps, "it would."

So far so good, thought Keith.

Dad put his paperwork onto the table with a flourish.

"Well," he said, grinning, "looks like the shop's a goer."

Mum gave him a delighted hug.

"Long way to go yet, of course," continued Dad, "but if we can keep the customers we've got so far, and get a few more as word spreads, I'd say we've got a successful shop on our hands."

Keith looked at Mum and Dad's smiling faces and felt like rushing outside and howling at the moon with joy. Except that it might disturb the snakes.

Dad's expression turned serious. He looked at Mum and Keith.

"If it wasn't for you two," he said, "I'd still be sitting in South London with a long face."

He kissed Mum and hugged Keith.

Keith glowed.

Dad turned to Tracy, grinning again. "When Keith started going on about Australia, I thought he'd gone bonkers. And then Keith's mum started and I thought she had too. But I came anyway and they were both right. It's paradise."

Keith looked at Tracy, expecting her to be pretty pleased with what Dad had just said about her country.

Instead she stared down at the table.

Then she said, "Thanks for tea, I'd better be going now."

• • •

Tracy didn't say anything as Keith walked with her down to the road.

She seemed in a strange mood.

Keith decided it was definitely indigestion and thought he'd better leave off telling her his plan about her parents until another time.

"Do you want to come down to our shop tomorrow for some free fish-and-chips?" he said. "There's something I want to talk to you about."

It wasn't until he'd said it that he remembered about the six pieces of cheese on toast. Could be an expensive talk. Hundred potatoes at least.

"No thanks," she said, not looking up.

Keith stared at her.

"Why not?"

" 'Cause I don't want to see you anymore."

Keith couldn't believe what he was hearing.

"Why not?"

She turned to him angrily.

" 'Cause you're a whinger."

Keith didn't know what that was but he felt sick in the stomach anyway.

"A what?"

"A whinger. Okay, we've got a few crocs and stingers around here, so what? That's not the end of the bloody world."

Keith realized what she meant. A whinger was a misery guts.

"You should learn to think positive," she said, "like your parents."

Keith opened his mouth but nothing came out.

"Instead of being a whinging Pom," Tracy said.

She walked away down the road.

After a bit she stopped and turned around.

"If you cheer up, give us a yell," she shouted.

Then she kept on walking.

Keith watched her. He realized his eyes were stinging. He rubbed both of them hard.

A mosquito must have bitten him on both eyelids.

● ● ●

Later, in bed, Keith felt better.

Mum and Dad are happy, he thought, and that's

the important thing. If they're happy, I'm happy.

He thought hard about whether he was happy.

He decided he was.

As he went to sleep, he tried not to think about what a great friend Tracy would have been.

Chapter Fourteen

Keith struggled awake.

A noise. On the roof of the caravan. Drumming. Rumbling. Thumping.

Snakes fighting?

A crocodile demanding to be let in?

Suddenly he knew what it was.

Rain.

Rain? Less than twelve hours ago, at the picnic, it had been searingly hot and there hadn't been a cloud in the sky.

He sat up in the darkness and pulled the curtain aside. Water was running down the outside of the window.

Think.

It could be a lawn sprinkler that had come on by

mistake. Perhaps that couple in the other caravan had had another fight and one of them had switched on the lawn sprinkler to sprinkle the other.

Keith peered over toward the shower block flood-light. In the arc of light he could see millions of drops of water falling from much higher up than a lawn sprinkler could sprinkle.

Rain.

Panic gripped him in the chest.

How could he do anything about rain?

Even if Tracy's parents were the best actors in the world they couldn't keep Mum and Dad shut up in their living room with the curtain drawn and the telly turned up forever.

Sooner or later Mum and Dad would step outside and there it would be. Gray skies. Gray buildings. Rain.

And gradually, drip by drip, Mum's forehead would pucker up and Dad's mouth would droop and the customers would stop coming and the shop would go broke and they'd be reduced to living on river banks and fighting with crocodiles over scraps of rotting takeaway chicken . . .

Keith clenched his fists.

Think positive.

If the sky was blue twelve hours ago, this must be a freak storm that's blown in from somewhere close that has rain. New Zealand. China. Somewhere like that.

And if it's blown in, thought Keith, stands to reason it'll blow out again. Probably by morning. When Mum and Dad wake up, the sky'll probably be blue again.

Not probably, it will be.

And Mum and Dad'll never know anything about it.

As long as they don't wake up now.

Keith held his breath and listened for their breathing. He couldn't hear anything except the drumming of the rain.

He felt on the floor next to his bed and found the candle and matches Mum had left there in case of emergency.

The candle flame lit up the caravan with a flickering yellow light.

Keith slipped out of bed and gently pulled aside the curtain that hung between Mum and Dad's bed and his.

Mum and Dad were both asleep.

Keith silently thanked the traffic of South London for turning them into such heavy sleepers.

But the rain on the roof was getting louder.

He couldn't chance it.

He found Mum's makeup bag, pulled out some tufts of cotton wool, rolled them into little balls, and carefully, gently, holding his breath, pushed one into one of Mum's ears.

She stirred slightly but stayed asleep.

He eased one into her other ear.

Dad was harder to do because he was on the other side of the bed.

Keith leaned over Mum, praying she wouldn't wake up and scream.

The first ball fell out of Dad's ear. Too small. He made bigger ones and eased them in.

Done.

He straightened up, heart pounding.

Now, check to make sure all the windows are closed.

That's when he remembered.

The side window in the shop.

He'd left it open so the shop wouldn't be too hot on Monday morning.

A night of pounding rain and the shop could be awash. Electrical wires could short-circuit. There could be a fire.

Another one.

He stood there, sweating, in the flickering candle-light.

I'll have to do it, he thought. I'll have to go and shut that window.

• • •

He was drenched to the skin before he got to the bottom of the caravan steps.

So much for Mum's showerproof raincoat.

He clasped it around him and sloshed across the

caravan park, slipping in the mud, eyes almost closed against the rain that beat on his head and shoulders like stones.

Blimey, he thought, this is worse than Worthing.

Then he reached the road.

For a moment Keith thought he'd been slammed in the back with a plank of wood, then he realized it was wind, screaming at him out of the darkness.

He staggered across the road and was only able to stop when he came up against the rough brick wall of the milk bar.

The rain was coming at him sideways now, and it felt like it was going to rip Mum's showerproof raincoat to shreds.

Keith squinted toward the beach.

All he could see were huge black waves pounding in, and foam being torn off them by the wind. Forget Worthing, he thought, this is worse than Scarborough.

He started to edge his way toward the shop at the other end of the street, eyes almost closed, the wind flattening him against the buildings as he struggled along.

Just past the hardware store he took another painful squint at the beach.

And saw the palm trees.

No longer were they leaning gracefully over the sand, they were thrashing around, fronds flailing in the black sky.

Suddenly it hit him.

Coconuts.

Fortunately it was only the thought that hit him. The coconut itself, the first of them, slammed against the post office wall in front of him and exploded.

Keith saw that the road was littered with coconuts. He heard others smashing into wood and glass.

Run, he thought. Leg it. Go back.

Then he remembered the shop.

If he didn't save the shop, there was no point in going back.

He hunched over and put his left arm up between him and the thrashing palm trees and edged forward.

A car with only one headlight and no windscreen went slowly past and the driver shouted something at him but Keith kept his head down and kept going.

Another coconut exploded against the wall in front of him.

A rubbish bin flew past his head.

Then he realized he was outside the swimwear boutique, which meant the next shop was theirs. He peered ahead. There it was.

He heard a screeching, groaning noise above him. He looked up and saw that the metal roof of the swimwear boutique was flapping around like a bedspread. It was coming down, toward him.

He flung himself against the wall as the sheets of tin crashed onto the road and were hurled along it, sparks flying.

And then suddenly the sheets of metal were in the air again and smashing, two and three at a time, into the front of the Paradise Fish Bar.

Keith watched the front of the shop disappear as the wind picked up the shattered glass and splintered wood and twisted metal and whipped them away.

He stared, numb, as the next gust, thundering into the open front of the shop, blew out every other window in the building.

He stood leaning against the swimwear boutique wall until the feeling came back into his body.

Paradise, he thought, looking at the dark, howling beach.

Rain and sand stung his eyes and he didn't care.

Twelve thousand miles, five airlines, seventy-three hours.

And all you had to do was make us happy.

"Thanks a lot, paradise," he yelled, "thanks a bleeding lot."

He yelled it again, screaming it into the wind with great sobs.

He was still yelling it when the real plank of wood slammed into him and everything went black.

Chapter Fifteen

First he saw Mum's face, looking down at him with sad red-rimmed eyes and wet cheeks and her forehead screwed up into so many crisscross lines he felt dizzy and sick trying to count them.

Then he saw Dad's face, frowning at him with dark eye bulges and droopy mouth creases that were darker and droopier than he'd ever seen before.

Then he saw Mitch Wilson, staring at him gloomily.

Then he saw Owen the milkman, looking at him sadly.

Then he saw Mr. Naylor, smiling at him with a thin mocking smile.

• • •

Then he woke up.

He was in a bed in a big bright room with lots of other beds in it.

Mum and Dad were sitting by the bed looking down at him.

Mum smiled, but her frown lines didn't go away.

Dad smiled too, but his droopy mouth creases just sort of stretched a bit.

They both hugged him.

Keith realized he had a headache.

"You're in hospital in Cairns, love," said Mum gently.

"You're going to be okay," said Dad.

They told him about the storm and how it was the edge of a cyclone that had gone back out to sea and how Raylene from the chemist's had found him lying unconscious on the road on her way to check that Mrs. Newman was okay and how the ambulance had taken hours to get him to Cairns because the road was blocked by trees and how he'd been asleep for eighteen hours and how worried they'd been about him.

Keith didn't say anything about the shop because they didn't, and he thought they looked depressed enough after sitting on those hard hospital chairs for eighteen hours.

• • •

He didn't mention it in the days that followed either.

He decided not to say much about anything.

He slept most of the time, and when he wasn't asleep he pretended he was so he wouldn't have to talk to Mum, who sat by his bed for several hours each day.

He wanted to talk, but not about the things he thought she'd want to talk about.

Like how coming to Australia was the worst thing they'd ever done and how they'd be going back to England as soon as Keith was better.

Anyway, she didn't have to tell him that out loud. He could tell from her face.

• • •

On the third day he couldn't stand it anymore and spoke.

"Nurse," he said, "could you get my mum a cushion?"

• • •

The only cheery person around was the doctor who stopped by the bed each day and shone a light into Keith's eyes.

"Good," he said every day, "good. I wish the plank of wood was coming along as well as you."

• • •

Then one day Mum came in looking much happier.

"Come on," she said, "we're going home today."

"Where's Dad?" asked Keith.

"At home," said Mum.

Great, thought Keith, Dad was so anxious to get back to Owen the milkman he couldn't even wait for us.

As Keith got dressed, he wondered if people who'd had a concussion were allowed to fly.

Perhaps they won't let me on the plane, he thought.

Them Mum would have to fly to England without him and he'd stay in Australia and become a wealthy sheep farmer with a property the size of Lewisham and then he could fly them back out.

Forget it, he thought gloomily. Champion boxers fly all the time and they get concussions on a weekly basis.

As he climbed into the ambulance, Keith briefly considered making a run for it but decided not to.

He didn't fancy being on the run in a country where the police carried guns and chewed chewing gum.

What's the point, he thought glumly. Lie back and let it happen.

He'd tried to make Mum and Dad happy and it hadn't worked out.

At least he'd have the consolation, when they

were living in a high-rise council flat and Dad was selling roof insulation and they were all miserable, of knowing he'd tried.

● ● ●

Keith wondered why the ambulance was taking so long to get to the airport. He tried to see if they were in a traffic jam but couldn't because of the frosted glass in the windows.

He looked at Mum, dozing in her seat, and remembered how her face had lit up when she first saw Orchid Cove.

And how she'd smiled when Dad had announced the shop was a goer.

Now, as she dozed, not only was her brow furrowed, her mouth was starting to droop too.

"Mum," he said.

She blinked awake. "Yes, dear?"

"I've got something to tell you."

"What's that, love?"

Keith took a deep breath. This wasn't going to be easy but it might just make her feel a bit better about having to leave.

"There are poisonous jellyfish," he said, "in the sea off Orchid Cove. And all up and down the coast."

"I know, love," she said.

Keith had already started telling her about the stonefish before he realized what she'd said.

She knew?

"Stonefish," she was saying, "that's right."

"And crocodiles in the rivers," he said, wondering if he was dreaming.

"I know," she said, smiling.

"And poisonous snakes," he said.

"That's right," she said.

"And spiders," he said suddenly desperate to find at least one horrible thing she didn't know about.

"Yes," she said.

"And coconuts that drop on your head and coral that infects your fingers," he shouted.

Mum bit her lip.

At last, thought Keith, something.

"I'm sorry, love," said Mum, "we should have told you about all those things."

Keith stared at her.

"But we knew how much you wanted this place to be perfect," she continued, "and we didn't want to make you miserable."

Keith tried to speak but couldn't.

"We should have told you," said Mum, "when Uncle Derek's travel agent friend told us."

"So, you mean," said Keith with difficulty, "you don't mind about them?"

Mum smiled and shook her head.

Keith's head was spinning.

"So if the cyclone hadn't come," he said, "we wouldn't be leaving?"

Mum looked at him with a puzzled little frown.

"Leaving?" she said. "We're not leaving."

Keith realized the ambulance had come to a stop and the driver had turned the engine off.

The doors opened and Keith could smell fish-and-chips.

He stepped out.

They were in Orchid Cove.

The ambulance was parked in front of the shop.

The shop had a new front on it.

Keith could smell the primer on the new timber. Through the new panes of glass he could see Dad at the fryer, hair curled up at the front.

Dad saw him and came out.

"Not a bad job, eh?" said Dad, pointing to the new front of the shop. "Mind you, I had expert help."

Out of the shop came Doug from the service station and Tracy's dad and Tracy, all eating fish-and-chips.

"G'day," said Tracy. "Your Dad's been telling me some of the things you used to get up to in England. Pretty wild stuff for a Pommy whinger."

Grinning, she offered him a chip.

Dazed, he took one.

"They reckon," Dad was saying, "that cyclones only come once in a blue moon, so we've decided not to worry about the next one till it happens."

Keith stared at Mum and Dad.

121

Grinning, they both gave him a hug.

"Okay," said Dad, "enough of this. There's a shop to be painted. We've saved you the top coat."

He handed Keith a paintbrush and a tin of paint.

Keith looked at the brush and the tin. Then he looked back at Mum and Dad, whose grins had become huge smiles of delight. They gazed at him, eyes shining.

Keith realized he was feeling something he hadn't felt for a very long time.

He was feeling happy.

He dipped the brush into the Tropical Mango Hi-Gloss.